# PIZZA IN PUSHKIN SQUARE

## What Russians Think About Americans and the American Way of Life

# VICTOR RIPP

SIMON AND SCHUSTER

New York   London   Toronto   Sydney   Tokyo   Singapore

**Simon and Schuster**
Simon & Schuster Building
Rockefeller Center
1230 Avenue of the Americas
New York, New York 10020

Designed by Chris Welch
Manufactured in the United States of America

1  3  5  7  9  10  8  6  4  2

Library of Congress Cataloging in Publication Data

Ripp, Victor.
Pizza in Pushkin Square : what Russians think about Americans and
the American way of life / Victor Ripp.
p.   cm.
Includes bibliographical references and index.
1. United States—Foreign public opinion, Soviet.   2. Public
opinion—Soviet Union—History—20th century.   3. Ripp, Victor—
Journeys—Soviet Union.   I. Title.
E183.8.S65R56   1990
973—dc20                                              90-39328
CIP
ISBN 0-671-66725-4

*To Gita, Nancy, and Alexandra*

# Contents

Foreword                                              9

  **one**    *Intimate Foes/Distant Friends*        13

  **two**    *Dreams of Capitalism*                 49

**three**    *Tracking the American Soul*          85

  **four**    *The Lay of the Land*                  117

  **five**    *Cultural Exchange*                     139

  **six**    *Passionate Etiquettes*                 179

*Afterword*                                          200

*Bibliographical Note*                               209

*Index*                                              213

# Foreword

During the year I spent in Leningrad in the early 1970s, I was invited
to a party in the home of a Soviet friend. It was a chaotic affair,
with excited conversations ranging through the three small rooms.
As the party wore on, its center of gravity wobbling, I found myself
blocked behind the kitchen table by a group declaiming poetry at
one another. Also trapped was an attractive brunette, and we began
to chat. She told me that her name was Tanya and that she was a
student at the Pedagogical Institute. I told her about New York
City and life in the West, and ended by inviting her to the ballet
on the following evening. She accepted without hesitation. In the
buoyancy of the moment I didn't give it a second thought, but I
might have realized that things were moving a bit fast.

When we met the next evening in front of the Kirov Theater,
Tanya was unexpectedly glum. While getting to our seats and waiting for the curtain, she hardly spoke. My efforts at conversation
were turned aside with sour grunts, and she didn't thank me for
the ice cream I bought for her during intermission. By the end of
the performance, I was convinced that Tanya had endured my
company only to get to see the ballet, and I escorted her home
grudgingly. But when we got to her door, she invited me in.

She directed me to the sofa in the center of the living room, then exited stage right without explanation. Left alone, I considered the possible outcomes of this odd encounter, wondering which signals the transcultural haze had made me miss. I was unprepared, however, for what happened next. The door opened and instead of Tanya there entered a young man with a wispy beard. I recognized him, dimly. He had been at the party. He had, now that I thought about it, been standing with Tanya before we struck up our conversation. During our chat he had hovered nearby.

He introduced himself, and sitting down next to me on the sofa began to prattle on about the rigors of the Leningrad winter, just as if this were the most natural of meetings. Soon, I noticed, he began to steer the conversation around to America, and to American jazz. He got me to agree it was a great art form, then began to itemize his favorite performers. I glanced toward the door, but Tanya was nowhere to be seen.

The young man leaned toward me, touched my arm for emphasis, and said, "I want to be your friend. I could tell you many things about Leningrad, take you places you would not otherwise see, introduce you to interesting people. And you—you could get me American jazz records?"

Given the sweet sound of Coltrane's sax, wasn't it worth risking the KGB's annoyance by associating with a foreigner? Entranced by Ella Fitzgerald's marvelous scat, should one ponder the morality of using a girlfriend as enticement? Tanya's friend wanted a piece of the America whose aura had somehow wafted in over the Iron Curtain, and he was going to get it at whatever price. At that moment, when I was reduced to being only a piece of a grandiose fantasy, I first recognized the power of America in Russia. I was being courted, but impersonally. I was wanted merely because of my nationality.

Even a quick stroll down Moscow's Gorky Street would make it clear that not all Russians view America with the enthusiasm of Tanya's boyfriend. Some condescend to it, others dislike it. But whatever the attitude, it is intensely held. America is very much on their minds. It's even in the language, this intimate awareness of America, in the widely used phrase *"Vot, on otkril Ameriku* (Look, he's discovered America)," which mocks the person who proclaims as a novelty what everyone already knows in thoroughgoing detail.

This is a bit surprising, since information about America has always been hard to come by. Before *glasnost,* the typical sources were Voice of America when it was not being jammed, bits of gossip picked up from an American tourist on Red Square, or, for those cunning enough, between-the-lines readings of the official press. Matters have noticeably improved, but there's a long way to go. Russians must still construct their America from a ragbag of data. This does not, however, stop them from describing our country as knowingly as if they had actually traversed it. Fueled by some passionate urge to comprehend America, they take flimsy pieces of evidence and hammer them together into opinions.

I've met more than a few Russians who claim to know America better than do Americans. Long-standing fascination with the subject has made them experts, often of a critical bent. We have dissipated our true heritage, they say, strayed from our best principles. There's a lot of fake piety in these protestations, but it's not all cant. Russians being different from us, the America they desire is different from the country we inhabit: the gap between the two seems genuinely to sadden them.

A *Pravda* correspondent recently traveled across America, stopping in Cooperstown, New York, with the intention of joining the crowds paying homage at the grave of James Fenimore Cooper, who is a great favorite in the Soviet Union. There were crowds, but they were streaming toward the Baseball Hall of Fame, a building that "was like a temple, with marble columns, and with gold and silver everywhere." Cooper's grave, when the correspondent finally found it, was modest and bleak and unvisited. He was greatly disappointed. He would have liked to find someone with whom to discuss *The Last of the Mohicans,* someone who was in touch with those true American values that were enshrined in his imagination. The correspondent entitled his book about his travels *A*

*Thousand Miles in Search of a Soul,* reflecting that mixture of plaintiveness and condescension with which many Russians regard this country. They think of us as one might of a young nephew who did not live up to his early promise. Russian opinions of America can be very unsettling. How can people living on the other side of the world in a society so different from ours come up with such self-confident conclusions?

Over the past fifteen years, I have been to the U.S.S.R. five times, on visits, official exchanges, even a glorious honeymoon in Leningrad. My nationality often influenced the encounters and conversations I had, the friendships I made, certainly more than in other foreign countries. But I never paid continual attention to Russian opinion of America, and indeed often tried to ignore it when confronted—the views tended to the stereotypic and outrageous, and had the power to set askew even those encounters that had begun promisingly. I always had before me as a cautionary example that evening with Tanya and her boyfriend, when in the space of a dizzying moment I was transformed from a simple traveler abroad into a piece of a myth. It had not been very pleasant.

But now I decided to go back and see how that myth was flourishing in the new Russia of Gorbachev. Things were changing, a world was a-borning, and the new order presumably included some reappraisals of America. There aren't many moments when it's possible to feel oneself riding the waves of history; being an American in Moscow in the late twentieth century was one of the rare opportunities. As much as possible, I decided, I would put myself in the way of Russians who were moving to comprehend an America that was suddenly available as never before. I packed up my notebooks, pocketed a bit of grant money from a friendly foundation, took a leave of absence from family and teaching obligations, and set off.

# one

# Intimate
# Foes/
# Distant
# Friends

I arrived in Moscow during an unusually mild stretch of fall, which served nicely to get me into the proper frame of mind. In this city, three consecutive sunny days in October is a miracle, and a tolerance for the miraculous is what I needed as I contemplated Russia. It was not the country I remembered from previous visits; if not an entirely new piece of work, then at least a much-revised edition, with a slant often far removed from the established Soviet style. Traces of America caught my eye. America was always the archenemy, and its influence was monitored as strictly as a virulent disease. Now, though there was still no mistaking Moscow for New York, bits of America were everywhere; they were on mundane display, with none of the fanfare that marks the special event.

The week of my arrival, *Biloxi Blues* and *King Kong* were playing in the local theaters. Improbably, Elvis Presley could be heard singing on the state-controlled radio; it was not so long ago that he was a propaganda target, an example of the decadence that breeds within capitalistic society. Over in the auditorium of the Hotel Rossiya, a touring company from New York was staging *Sophisticated Ladies;* I found it incongruous that this example of Broadway glitz was on display in a building whose grandiose style makes it a virtual icon of Soviet self-satisfaction, but no one else seemed to mind. There was a McDonald's just off the city's main drag, and people were still talking about the Astro Pizza truck that recently circulated through the streets around the Kremlin—though what they were saying is that buying a piece of America at two rubles a slice was a bit steep.

In the Hotel National where I put up, Americans were everywhere. I met them serially in the ornate, turn-of-the-century dining room, a new American every day, thanks to the Russian practice of filling up all the places at one table before allowing anyone to sit at the next. No one would explain the reason for this practice, but it was inalterable. My annoyance at being ordered about by the sullen maître d' was balanced by the pleasures of sociological curiosity. Before me passed a whole parade of classic American characters, from the Californian dressed as if for a day's sailing to a ramrod-straight Maine teacher. One couple never appeared without a jar of decaffeinated coffee, setting it on the table to act as a talisman against the evil spirits of the native cuisine.

Most conspicuous of all were the businessmen. One or two had been coming for many years to try to make deals, enduring long, bleak days in hotel rooms watching telephones that never rang; they were here in Gorbachev's promised land to claim the fruits of wandering through the Brezhnevian desert. But most of the businessmen were first-timers who had caught the scent of a lucrative new market. Each morning they all appeared, well-scrubbed and attired in pinstripes, briefcases in hand. I often saw them again at night in the hotel's foreign currency bar, buying drinks for the $100-a-night hookers and bawling college marching songs. A venture capitalist from Chicago explained to me that he was only "networking": the flashy blonde who had been at his table was in fact his agent, passing along information that business rivals had let drop in unguarded moments. It was hard to imagine what Russians thought of all this. They of course had heard of our pursuit of money, but I doubt that they pictured it in all its colorful detail.

It is this closer focus that marks Russians' new perspective on

American life. They have been aware of us for centuries, but opinion was always formed at a distance. There was an intellectual as well as a physical remove. It is telling that Russians routinely referred to America as the "transatlantic republic"—which not only suggests vast geographical distance but also, in the substitution of a fancy nickname for our proper name, conjures up a cloud of exoticism. America stimulated conjecture, and, indeed, Russians devised an image of us without knowing very much about our everyday life. They addressed themselves to the broader outlines. But now we are here in person, all on display.

On the second day after my arrival, I was sitting in the hotel lobby and diligently working my way through *Pravda*, when I was startled by a loud, unmistakably American-accented yelp. "Oh, I would kill, just kill, to be able to speak Russian so I could explain myself to all these lovely people." Promenading through the lobby was a man wearing a bright red warm-up suit, with spangled sunglasses pushed back on his blond curly hair. A small entourage, of only slightly less stunning appearance, was deployed behind him. People in the lobby abruptly stopped what they were doing, distracted just as if a bright comet with its tail of waning light were passing through. I later learned that the man was the "television personality" Richard Simmons, famous in America for his exercise programs, which are broadcast every morning. He was in Moscow as part of a cultural exchange (though surely Russia has no equivalent to offer in return), and when I saw him he had just returned from Gorky Park. On the plaza just beyond the park's entrance, he had led a group of young Muscovites through an hour of aerobics to the accompaniment of rock and roll and his own chirpy exhortations.

The effect of America's intrusions is not always easy to measure, but here was one for which I had a calibrating device. On one of my previous visits to Moscow, I had gone early one morning for a walk in Gorky Park and on that same plaza had come across some one hundred members of a Pioneer youth group engaged in those synchronized movements—half gymnastics, half proletarian mime

15

show—that the Ministry of Physical Culture ordained for younger citizens. It should have been ridiculous, but for some reason I was entranced. For an hour I stood in the morning chill and watched the oddly mechanical movements. They were so solemn, all those ten- and eleven-year-olds, so absolutely concentrated on their activity. What at first glance seemed silly became in its unironical performance something like a ritual. Richard Simmons' strutting and posing had not taken place in a void; they were played out against the backdrop of a confident and serviceable existing culture.

Indeed, all of America's offerings, the powerful expressions of our contemporary life as well as the merely fatuous, will be scrutinized through a native prism, not accepted innocently. The only question is this: As America becomes increasingly visible in Russia, will the long-standing myths surrounding our image retain any force at all, or will they be totally dispelled by the accumulated force of more pragmatic evidence? Will Richard Simmons and his exercise routine completely outweigh the marvelous stories about the transatlantic republic?

National images are notoriously difficult to track. They are not fixed and final like paintings hung in a museum, but change with the times. There are limits, however. Only certain additions can fit into what is already there. Russia's image of America, as it happens, particularly resists too much tampering. It has tenacity bred into it.

Signs of the pedigree are visible in one of the first eyewitness reports about America by a Russian. Pavel Svinin, who served as secretary to the consul general of Russia in Philadelphia from 1810 to 1815, was eager to explain the New World to his compatriots back home. "No two countries," he wrote, "bear a more striking resemblance than Russia and the United States. . . ." Though Svinin's argument had some weak links (he claimed that republican America and tsarist Russia were equally models of democracy), his discovery of a convergence between the two countries had an enduring history. Throughout the nineteenth century, many Russians found that the best angle from which to look at America was across the vista of their own experiences. They spied out similarities where none would have thought to look, and some even claimed to have discovered a shared destiny.

Though substantial differences were swept aside in the rush to find parallels, the theory was not spun wholly out of the air; there was supporting evidence, though it had to be couched in ingenious terms. America was at the beginning of its history; Russia, it was argued, was so backward that it had no choice but to begin history anew. For both countries the future lay waiting to be made. America and Russia were equally well-situated for such a project, at a distance from the contamination of a Europe that was on the brink of exhaustion. An expanding frontier in both Russia and America confirmed the idea of the two as growing giants, eager to test their maturing energies. In 1857 that most astute political observer Alexander Herzen remarked, "Both countries, starting from different sides, traverse vast spaces to reach the shores of the Pacific Ocean, the Mediterranean of the future." The words implied not only geographical expansion but an efflorescence of the national spirit. Physical expanse engendered optimism. Common wisdom in both America and Russia had it that one could always pick up stakes and try again in still unoccupied land. It's no accident that *Huckleberry Finn* was a favorite with the Russian reading public—Huck's decision to shuck off the constricting conventions of Hannibal, Missouri, and to "light out for the territories" was one that Russians could easily comprehend.

Russians' admiration for America was never unqualified. There was much in our way of life they disliked, and at the beginning of the twentieth century two new circumstances gave the criticism a sharper edge. Where once America had been an ally (acting to help curb British expansionism), its Far East policies now made it a rival. And where once America had been a model of a progressive society, a new generation of Russian socialists now considered it politically retrograde. Nevertheless the sense of an essential connection remained. It was, indeed, in this period that a whole new range of American activities began to attract attention. From labor practices to architecture, from literature to consumer services, America was held up as the country Russia most approximated and that it should copy more fully. In a widely praised poem, Alexander Blok imagined Siberia transformed into a replica of America. "Now over the empty steppes there brightens / My America, My new-risen star," he rhapsodized, and his audiences applauded.

After the Bolshevik Revolution references to America became combative and sometimes nasty. Comparisons were still drawn, but often just for the chance to make them invidious. "Just you wait, bourgeois! There will be a New York in Tetyushi. . . ." proclaimed the poet Vladimir Mayakovsky, insisting that even a dreary one-horse town on the Volga could be transformed by Soviet methods into something surpassing capitalism's greatest pride. If America still provided a model, it was one that had to be overhauled and improved for use in Russia; if the two countries were mirror images, there would be attractive variations in the Russian reflection. But scorn, especially the huffing-and-puffing variety exhibited by Mayakovsky, is pretty far from outright dismissal. America was still a compelling standard, still invoked regularly as a model. Traveling through our western states in 1931, the writer Boris Pilnyak found the town of Kingman, Arizona, to be just like his Transvolga hometown; the prairies reminded him of the Ukraine; and as his train went through the Rockies he insisted that "the landscape beyond the window was absolutely identical [*toch v toch*] to that of Central Asia." Pilnyak's purpose was to prove the Soviet Union's superiority in all things, even the scenery, but he found no better way than to begin by admitting a similarity. Even when American reality was deficient, it was plotted along lines Russians found utterly familiar.

The Soviet regime has sometimes endorsed the idea of a Russian-American convergence but more often discouraged it. To a significant degree, however, official policy has been irrelevant. The popular imagination lies beyond the reach of decree. It plucks its proofs from the cultural buzz, sometimes giving as much weight to the trivial as the stupendous. Thus, the fact that eighteenth- and early-nineteenth-century Russian fur traders had outposts on a stretch extending from the Aleutian Islands to Fort Ross, California, strikingly suggests an intermingling of national destinies, and yet it may be one that is no more compelling to the average Russian than the information that roller coasters in 1930s America were called "Russian hills" while those in Russia were called "American hills." The popular imagination does not make fine distinctions.

When the writers Ilya Ilf and Evgeny Petrov toured America in 1935, they met a man in Dearborn, Michigan, whom they described this way: "His eyes are set close together, the prickly eyes of a peasant. As a matter of fact, he looks very much like a sharp-nosed Russian peasant, a self-made inventor who suddenly shaved off his beard and put on an English suit of clothes." It would seem that the Russian urge to refashion America along familiar lines can go no further than this: Henry Ford, American to the bone, almost primordially native in occupation and in appearance, is here trans-formed into a *muzhik*. There were good reasons for Ilf and Petrov to think fondly of Ford, since he had provided aid to Soviet industry in a time of crisis; but it is distinctly odd that they cast their affection in the form of giving Ford a Russian lineage. Their turn of phrase, lightly humorous but telling nevertheless, is an aspect of the nation's free-floating fantasy, a dream that projects a Russia and an America that are somehow akin; the hostility that has sparked up between us has often been ferocious, but many Russians believe that it is of the sort that touches all intimate relations.

Russia's image of America has always been shot through with such contradictory features. America is the familiar Other, the an-tagonistic friend, the model to be copied but also transcended, and (especially to those at odds with their own government) a distant force somehow capable of altering the immediate landscape. In other words, Russia's image of America includes Russia's image of itself. Altering what they think of America would require Russians to alter what they think of Russia, which is an onerous task. There-fore even though our way of life is open to Russian scrutiny as never before, there is reason to think that our long-standing image will persist a while longer. It is held together by the tensions of paradox.

The morning after I saw Richard Simmons promenading in the hotel lobby, I went to the main post office on Gorky Street to order a telephone call home to New Jersey. As in most Soviet public places, there was a crowd of people jockeying for position. Experience has taught the citizens that whatever they have come for—food, tickets, visas—may without warning be declared unavailable for the rest of the day or forever. The crowd pressed forward nervously, but without ever forgetting the lessons of civic decorum that socialism has taught. I managed to get through to the international desk, placed my order with a clerk who may or may not have listened to what I said, and received in return a scrap of paper with a scrawl on it. Trying to decipher this, the one halfway substantial piece in a hopelessly chaotic process, I at first did not notice that a young woman was tentatively circling me, apparently trying to decide whether to approach. She seemed to sigh, then plunged forward with resolve.

She had heard me place my order, hence knew I was an American, and she wanted me to help her. Americans in Moscow are fair game, constantly being solicited for all sorts of favors, many of them illegal. But this young woman had an unfocused, desperate manner, hardly the look of a black marketeer. I let her guide me to a corner bench.

She was from Kiev, she told me, only visiting Moscow for a few days. She had come to the post office planning to call some American friends in Chicago, but at the last minute had decided on a letter instead. Her English was very weak, however, only a couple of phrases really. She wanted me to translate her words and to write out a proper letter. It seemed a harmless request and I wondered why she seemed so anxious. I took the offered pen and paper and began to write as she spoke.

"Dear John and Linda, it was so good seeing you on your visit. We so much liked showing you around, and are happy you liked our Kiev. We look forward to your coming again soon. But next time I will have to meet you alone. A terrible thing has happened. My husband has been arrested."

I paused, turning to look at her. The paragraph of neutral sentences that I was composing hardly seemed the right form for her tragic story. I felt awkward, and suggested that perhaps she needed to find someone else to help her. She looked at me imploringly. I bent back to my task.

Her husband, as young as she, had come to Moscow a week ago. Outside one of the larger hotels he had approached an American tourist and had offered to sell her a lacquered box of purportedly native handicraft. It's a common enough transaction, with advantages to both sides—the tourist gets the thrill of experiencing a bit of the real Russia, off the beaten track of the official itinerary, and the Russian makes some money. But it's also illegal. Though the police usually only shoo the hustlers away, the husband was arrested and taken off to jail. Since then, the wife had only managed to see him for thirty seconds, as he was being transferred between holding cell and prison.

"Why did she do it, that stupid American lady?" the young woman suddenly wailed with such poignancy that a few of the other patrons glanced in our direction. "How could she not know that she had only to deny that my husband had sold her anything? Then the police would have done nothing. Now my husband is going to jail for three years. And the American lady? She will go back to the United States and never think about it. John and Linda are lawyers—perhaps they will be able to do something."

I finished writing the letter for her and we parted. Though I couldn't imagine what the letter might accomplish, she thanked me as if I had performed a great service.

It was not till after I got back to my hotel room that I began to think more clearly about the episode. Though it was a pure-bred Soviet drama—the state's absolute power, a prison term, a devoted wife cursing the heavens—it was the role of Americans that was most striking. Like the whims of the gods which had dire consequences for mortals, the casual acts of Americans were inexplicably magnified, causing great misfortune but also promising salvation. My part had been that of the poet-scribe, who by his command of words helps to avoid disaster.

The importance that Russians impute to Americans was familiar to me from my earlier stays, during the pre-Gorbachev era. We were often made to feel we were the sole fragile link with the outside world. Even when doing nothing more than providing an old copy of *Newsweek* or passing along a greeting from a mutual friend in the States, our actions seemed to shimmer with high significance. The risk of running afoul of the authorities was in actuality small, but the unspoken credo was that we were all joined in facing down an oppressive regime. Newspaper reporters, academics on exchanges, government officials—we came as innocents and left as old Russian hands, having metamorphosed with no more effort than it took to stroll down the avenue, and often to as little purpose. The incident in the post office suggested the rules of the game hadn't changed all that much. America was still being made to play the extravagant roles Russians assigned to it.

The role in this case—powerful friend of the oppressed—seemed especially dated. With all the liberalizing changes that have lately come to the Soviet Union, is there any need for a foreign savior? On the streets of Moscow, where the *militsya* and the citizenry are still locked in their old struggles, the weaker camp is not above calling for American reinforcements, if only because that was often the strategy in the past.

How Russians look at America is very much influenced by how they think we look at them. For centuries Russia has worried about the face it shows the world. "What news on the Rialto?" Shakespeare's Venetian asks, displaying the curiosity men everywhere have about the goings-on in their own cities. "Gorky Street," a Muscovite is more likely to say, "what news of it on the Rialto?" Always lagging in material goods, almost always a bit backward culturally, Russia has a long-standing inferiority complex. The belligerence it periodically exhibits is in some measure anxiety about its own powers. The emblematic national posture is a defensive crouch with a nervous over-the-shoulder glance.

A lot of the edginess can be traced back to the postrevolutionary period, when Russian sensitivities were rubbed raw. The new regime, eager to have its legitimacy endorsed, applied for equal standing in the community of nations; but the community of nations demurred. International law holds that any regime with de facto power deserves accreditation, but a communist regime was apparently too hard to stomach, international law or not. Efforts to establish diplomatic relations with the United States were met by demands that the Soviets first pay the debts incurred by the tsarist regime, that they make compensation for property lost during the revolution, and that they refrain from subversive propaganda abroad. The Soviets characterized the idea that it pursued subversive policies as paranoiac, and added that any financial claims had to take into account the damages done by Americans taking part in the Allied Expeditionary Force's 1918 incursion onto sovereign soil.

Though the negotiating positions appear symmetrical, Russia was always the more eager party. "We have never concealed our regret," Foreign Minister Maksim Litvinov stated in 1928, "at the absence of official relations between us and the transatlantic republic with which we have no conflicts and foresee none." The comment was ingenuous in several ways, but it does sketch the balance of enthusiasms. The Soviet Union played the role of determined suitor, the United States that of the coy and aloof damsel. It was a case where the conventions of diplomatic terminology echoed psychological truth, "nonrecognition" conveying some of the hurt that results when the extended hand is met by a blank stare. Formal relations were not established until 1933, long after Russians expected it, and even then the agreement was hedged around with unusual provisos. (Roosevelt's administration demanded, for example, explicit guarantees of religious freedom for American nationals on Soviet soil, as if the spiritual purity of the embassy staff was at risk.) Why did it all take so long? Why could America not give Russia its full due?

During my stay in Moscow, I heard this note of injured pride many times, modulated to fit a wide range of topics. "Which of our films are most popular in the States?" a Moscow director asked me, smuggling in the implication that Americans see enough Russian films to make distinctions. Maneuvering through the dense and erratic traffic on Kalininsky Prospect, a taxi driver turned almost all the way around in his seat to inquire, "Our basketball team, the one that beat your fellows in the Olympics, are any of them good enough to be stars in the National Basketball Association?" A teacher wanted to know when Americans would begin to study Russian culture in earnest. "We defeated the Mongols and kept them out of Europe," she practically screamed at me. "We know all about American history and your country doesn't even realize that Russia once saved all of Western civilization." America's slights seem even worse because Russians suspect they are not malicious. Other nations, the French and the Germans, for example, may be condescending, but they at least are aware of that which they dismiss. Americans, Russians believe, cannot concentrate long enough to form an opinion. It's hard, listening to them present proofs of our inattention, not to be persuaded by their case.

A friend, a history professor at Moscow University, offered two exhibits for the prosecution. "It's the constancy of ignorance that is so disturbing," he said mournfully. The first exhibit was the visit of anarchist Peter Kropotkin to Boston in 1901. Kropotkin brought news of the Russian student movement that seemed about to topple the tsar; he found that Harvard students were less interested in the political protests of their Kievan counterparts than in their own rebellion against the "mutton monotony" of the food served in Memorial Hall. The second exhibit was the visit of writer Victor Nekrasov, seventy-five years later, to another Ivy League university. Nekrasov found that interest in Russia had hardly increased. "The American (factory worker, office worker, student) is not very

much given to cogitating or philosophizing. This is not primitive-
ness, as some think, and not mental laziness; it is rather, I would
say, a kind of infantilism . . . or, as one high-spirited Columbia
student said to me, 'We don't like it when they fill our heads with
all sorts of garbage.' "

America's attitude dismays Russians, but they tend to describe
it with humor. Anecdotes and jokes about our parochialism
abound, almost constituting a genre of their own. The poet Vladimir Mayakovsky can hardly keep a straight face as he relates the
questions put to him by a United States consular official in connection with a visa application in 1925. " 'Moscow? Is that in Poland?' 'No,' I replied, 'it's in the U.S.S.R.' No reaction." Some
Russians insist that even visiting Americans, who have Russia
spread out before them, are hardly able to comprehend what sur-
rounds them. There's the one about the famous engineer from Ford
who thought the river outside his hotel was the Oka, which actually
lies well off to the south, or the tourist in Leningrad who kept
asking to be taken to St. Petersburg—many Russians have a story
like this to tell, adding their bit to the national effort to deflect
insult.

Jokes about fatuous Americans go only so far. Exasperation with
our indifference always threatens to break through. It manifests
itself suddenly and in the most unexpected places, a feeling too
strong to be kept in check forever. For example, the standard Soviet
history of American-Russian relations, by Professor N. N. Bolkhovitinov, is a sober, scholarly work written in a dispassionate
style, but even here the reserve occasionally falters. Of the refusal
of the United States Congress to send a diplomatic mission to
Moscow in 1809 it is said, "The thrifty congressmen considered
the mission too expensive and unnecessary. (This did not prevent
them, at the same time, from sending a mission to Rio de Janeiro.)"
In describing John Quincy Adams, who served in Moscow as
America's minister plenipotentiary, the tone becomes even more
irritable. "It is regrettable that [Adams] had neither the persistence
nor the patience to study the Russian language. He certainly had

enough time for this task. . . . He was in Russia as minister for four and a half years, not to mention his 1780–82 stay in St. Petersburg. During those years he took detailed notes on the weather, made lists of correspondents and expenditures and constructed endless lists of the weights and measures used in Russia." What is the point of stressing the common destiny of two countries when one of them hardly gives serious consideration to the other?

Soviet views of American life are often slanted in a way that tries to redress the balance. Special emphasis is given to those exceptional Americans who paid proper attention to Russia. John Reed, Scott Nearing, Floyd Dell, Joseph Freeman—these and other figures who to us seem peripheral are moved to center stage. Albert Maltz and Erskine Caldwell are honored writers. Lincoln Steffens has a status greater by far than most Americans would concede to him, and Meredith Wilson, whose 1961 novel *Meeting at a Far Meridian* celebrates Soviet-American scientific cooperation, has been acclaimed a genius. Van Cliburn is still treated as a major artist by Russians; once an American pianist wins the Tchaikovsky Competition in Moscow, he emanates an aura that never dims.

A visit is especially appreciated. Warren Harding's manipulation of the famine relief program in 1921 was bitterly condemned ("famine diplomacy," Litvinov called it), but he gained a measure of redemption by making a personal appearance; the Soviet of People's Commissars sent him a letter of gratitude, ignoring for the moment his attempts to use food to wring out political concessions. Russians never loved Richard Nixon, but his journeys to Moscow brought him respect. Mark Twain's stock, already high, rises still higher because he once stopped at Yalta (and proclaimed his visit to the world in *The Innocents Abroad*). Russians have had their arguments with Arthur Miller, John Dos Passos, Theodore Dreiser, but they remember with affection that these men have passed this way. A visit, whatever else it may be, constitutes presumptive evidence that someone at least knows where to find Russia on the map.

Among the very favorite Americans is Benjamin Franklin. (A

recent biography had an initial printing of 100,000 copies.) Franklin's style endears him to Russians; his disdain for pomp, his plain dress, and his practicality are qualities they value. In broad outline he is, indeed, a recognizable Russian type, the *chudak,* the eccentric of great accomplishment. *Poor Richard's Almanac* was the first work by an American to be translated into Russian, in 1784, and there is no doubt that Russians of the day saw a kindred sensibility at work.

But Franklin is a hero not only because of his character. Franklin entered into correspondences with Russians, he met Russians, he— to put it in a word—acknowledged Russia. The connection, it is true, started a bit fatuously, with Franklin's participation in Catherine the Great's project for a universal dictionary. The empress subscribed to the misguided theory that all languages had a common source, and she wanted examples from Shawnee to match against the Russian. She wrote to Lafayette, who passed the request on to Franklin with the comment that ". . . the Empress, although I think to very little purpose, sets a great value upon it." Franklin complied as best he could (thus sealing what might be called the first Russian-American cultural exchange), but the project predictably came to nothing.

More substantial communications followed. Franklin corresponded with the St. Petersburg Academy of Sciences about theories of electricity. Soviet historians have suggested that Franklin was influenced by the research of Mikhail Lomonosov, Russia's great autodidact, but that is unlikely. Lomonosov's main theory about electricity was absolutely wrong and his experiments were sometimes wildly misconceived—one of his collaborators died while fiddling with a "thunder machine" installed on a roof. ("He died a beautiful death," Lomonosov averred.) But if Franklin did not follow Lomonosov's path, he did keep abreast of his efforts. Typically, Franklin's newspaper, *The Pennsylvania Gazette,* carried a full report about the "thunder machine" accident.

Always happy to promote relations between the two countries, Franklin persuaded the American Philosophical Society of Philadelphia to offer membership to Princess Dashkova, the director of the St. Petersburg Academy. Nominating Franklin in turn for the St. Petersburg Academy, Dashkova noted in her petition, "He bears me enough friendship and respect to propose me as a member of this respected and already famous Philosophical Society of Philadelphia." The motif of reciprocity sketched by Dashkova has been carried forward by Russian historians who have treated Franklin. One remarks, "At a time when Western Europe was doubtful about, even scornful of Franklin's experiments, Russians greeted them with honor." Which is to say, Russia treats with respect those who treat it with respect. In assessing their relations with America, Russians constantly search for such a balance point; disequilibrium triggers anxiety about being slighted.

Over the years, America's behavior has rarely satisfied Russia's deep desire for perfect reciprocity. When examples are found, Soviet historians tend to make much of them. This holds true even for actions involving the tsarist regime, which normally is scorned as the corrupt old order that communism transcended. One of the instances of American-Russian cooperation most frequently invoked is, indeed, an episode during the American Civil War. In 1862, the Imperial Navy dispatched three ships to visit Northern ports. The squadron's appearance had symbolic weight, dispelling the appearance of the North's diplomatic isolation. The visit heartened Northerners during a difficult period, and they turned out to meet the Russians with joy and public celebrations. But as a military operation it didn't amount to much. The Russians had strict orders to avoid being drawn into the hostilities. (They had, in fact, set sail from their Baltic ports because England was becoming increasingly belligerent in that part of the world.) The officers and sailors spent most of their time in New York attending parties in their honor and carousing. The composer Rimsky-Korsakov, who was then a naval cadet, noted, "How did we pass the time? We visited restaurants and lounged about, eating and occasionally drinking. An extra quantity of wine came somehow to be consumed rather often." Alternatively, they frequented prostitutes. Add to these facts the mental instability of the squadron's commander—once, in a fit of rage, Admiral Lesovsky had bitten off the nose of a sailor who did not obey his orders quickly enough—and the whole enterprise begins to seem a bit inane. But all this has not caused Soviet historians to qualify the pride with which they view it. Here was a moment when America was wise enough to appreciate Russia's goodwill. After the war was over, Undersecretary of the Navy Gustavus Fox headed a mission to St. Petersburg as a gesture of gratitude. That, a Russian would say, is the way it should be.

The key test of proper behavior—a category of its own, really—is World War II. Even for those Russians who are generations removed from it, this event is at the center of their view of the world. How other nations acted during the years 1939–45 is the standard for judging their worth today. At what point did they take up arms, how forcefully did they press the cause, how much support did they extend to Russia? By these standards, America gets mixed grades. As Russia's ally, it provided war matériel at a critical juncture, and American troops fought and died for the same ends as Russian troops. In those days when survival hung in the balance, every cooperative gesture could have great resonance: many Russians still recall the 1943 broadcast from America of Arturo Toscanini conducting the NBC orchestra in Shostakovich's *Leningrad Symphony*. With Russia embattled and in ruins, America had shown solidarity. That counts for a lot.

But the debit entries for America are many. It is true that America provided aid through the Lend-Lease program, but it was late in coming, and stingy when it came. Americans shed blood, but not until 1941. There is still a lot of anger about the Second Front. Why did it take so long to relieve German pressure on Russia? Churchill was the chief villain, it is widely believed, but America connived in his decision. It only fuels Russians' annoyance to hear Americans claim that Normandy was the decisive battle of the war—that honor belongs to Stalingrad, hands down.

Such lapses and deceits add up to a damning bill of indictment, but something less easily calculable also disturbs Russians—they believe Americans have not properly honored their wartime suffering. During the war it was common practice to depict Americans as paragons of insensitivity, men and women so smug in their own comfort that they could not comprehend the misfortune of others. *The Red Star,* the paper of the Soviet armed forces, regularly carried articles in this vein; in one typical dispatch from 1943 a correspondent addressed the average American who thought he could get through the war "without soiling your hands," who was sitting in a comfortable well-lit home while "your wife is serving dinner and your five-year-old daughter, sitting on your lap, is telling you about the events of the day." A year later, United States military participation could hardly be denied, but many Russians still believed that Americans failed to comprehend the horrors that war unleashed. *The Red Star* described the American soldiers who were stationed in Russia as ". . . tall happy guys in leather coats with bright scarves tied around their necks . . . their merry, curious eyes, their quick speech, their love of buying endless souvenirs. More than anything else, they like the toy store; they go in and buy painted wooden hand-crafted toys, wooden bowls painted with bright flowers—all kinds of amusing trifles."

Remarkably, the tradition of showing up American obtuseness persisted well into the 1980s, at almost the same level of shrillness. Even today, in the age of Gorbachev, one finds many traces of the old attitude. Soviet correspondents in the United States, who somehow seem regularly to encounter Americans with foolish opinions about the war, are among those who press the case vigorously. Traveling through the Midwest, a *Pravda* correspondent reported meeting a gas-station attendant who believed that America had entered the war first and thereafter carried the brunt of the burden. "Could it be that you really lost more than a million men?" the man asks incredulously and "becomes thoroughly disoriented" when told that the number of casualties was actually twenty million. In a New York luncheonette the correspondent encountered a woman who complained to him about wartime deprivations on the home front, when it was impossible to have chicken on the dinner table every night. The lurid revealing detail is typical for the genre (the woman in the luncheonette "poured rich cream into her coffee" as she spoke) and so is the intense pitch of Russian scorn.

The unwillingness to let the matter rest even now, four decades after the war, borders on obsession. There are, indeed, many of the classical symptoms, including the belief that the past might easily have taken a different course. Mixed in with the anger is an element of acute disappointment—the American attitude toward the war was and is reprehensible, but it need not have been. Those years were an opportunity for Americans to see Russia close up, and to honor it, if only they could have brought themselves to do the right thing.

One instance of Americans behaving as they should occurred right down the street from my hotel, on the day when news of the German surrender reached Moscow. A large crowd gathered in front of the building that then housed the United States embassy, and began cheering. In response, the embassy staff hung out the Soviet flag alongside the Stars and Stripes. George Kennan, who was chargé d'affaires at the embassy, mounted the pedestal of a column and shouted in Russian, "Congratulations on the day of victory. All honor to the Soviet allies." This caused a new transport of enthusiasm. Any American venturing onto the street was hoisted into the air and passed along on the friendly hands of the crowd.

Such displays of requited affection, when Russia honored America and was honored in return, are cherished. They conform to those extravagant ideas about our common destinies: in those wartime years, we were allies, changing the world together. The feelings such a vision stirs can be strong, but they never obliterate the sense that for much of the war America was only a lukewarm ally, indifferent to Russian suffering. Russians' anger and affection toward us are stirred into a volatile mixture.

During one of my earlier stays in Russia, I took a trip to Kolomenskoe, on the outskirts of Moscow. It was a fine summer day, and after spending an hour examining the famous church I bought a bottle of wine and some good bread and sat down on a hill to enjoy the view of the winding Moscow River. An elderly man with a dignified air struck up a conversation with me about the church's architecture. He kept glancing surreptitiously at my wine, and I passed him the bottle. After gulping down a drink, he beckoned a friend, a short, red-faced fellow with a plunging limp, to join us. As we passed the bottle back and forth, we chatted idly and watched the sun beat down on the river. It was a pleasant way to spend an afternoon. Then I mentioned that I was American. A shadow passed over the shorter man's face as he took this in. Turning red with anger, he began slapping at his damaged leg and cursing General Eisenhower and President Roosevelt—and also me. He seemed incensed that I had hoodwinked him with my conviviality. He would never, he shouted, knowingly have broken bread with a son of a perfidious nation. I had planned a tour of the grounds, but the man would not stop harassing and threatening me, and I finally had no choice but to cut my outing short and return to the city.

Has *perestroika* been able to restructure the edginess about America's sincerity? I reminded myself of the common wisdom that the younger generation is always in the vanguard when a country changes its perspective, and arranged to visit a Moscow secondary school in order to talk to the students about America.

A glance at the history textbook that was used in this school was not encouraging. Though there has been a lot of talk about rewriting the curriculum, so far little has been done actually. From what I read, it seemed that the same old scores were still being settled, the same old wounds still being picked at. This was especially true in the textbook's treatment of World War II. The textbook notes, "The casualties suffered by Americans were seventy times less than the human losses of the Soviet Union." Americans did provide material aid through the Lend-Lease program, but not enough and after too much delay. The claim that America played a major role in the war effort by serving as "the arsenal of democracy" is laughed out of court as a fantasy of bourgeois historians. "American monopolies squeezed enormous profits from military production." On the vexing question of the opening of a Second Front to relieve German pressure in the east, the textbook allows that the Americans were less hesitant than the English. "The chief opponent of an advance into Europe was Churchill." But the United States complied, and with few objections. Both countries, it is held, were happy to have Russia carry the burden of the fighting, hoping this would make communism too weak to be a major factor in the postwar era. (The textbook, which has a knack for the pithy quotation, cites then-Senator Harry Truman's comment that he hoped Russia and Germany "would bleed themselves dry" in an internecine struggle.) The validity of these assertions aside— and most rang more or less true—the querulous tone was remarkable so late in the game. It suggested a boxer who won't stop throwing punches long after the final bell has sounded, the fans departed and the stadium locked shut. I cheered myself with the thought that Russian students might pay no more attention to their textbooks than do American students, and headed for the school.

When I got there, the principal, a stout woman in her fifties with startlingly red hair, was there to greet me at the entrance. We made our way upstairs through the milling students who were shoving and joking in the manner that marks the end of the school day everywhere in the world. But their stark uniforms and their extreme deference to teachers made a singular impression. Since I could not politely frame a question about student subservience to authority, I instead asked the principal about the uniforms. "It's required," she said, "though the boys don't usually wear ties. That is in honor of your visit."

Thus made aware that I had added to the students' burdens, I let myself be led into a large, well-scrubbed classroom on the second floor. There were about fifty students inside, fourteen- and fifteen-year-olds who filled every seat. Introducing me, the principal emphasized the significance of the occasion. My visit, she declared, was a sign of the times, evidence of improving East-West relations. I had come in an effort to understand Russian life better, just as they were trying to understand American life. And so on.

By the time she finished, a wall of decorum had been raised between me and the students, and I looked for ways to dismantle it. I declined the principal's invitation to sit behind the imposing desk at the front of the room. I would stand, I said, unbuttoning my jacket and loosening my tie and addressing the class with joking good humor. To my surprise, my democratic style did not play very well. A compliment to the national basketball team was met with blank looks, a wisecrack about my Russian ancestry got silent smirks. The mood was not antagonistic, but neither was this an easy audience.

I got down to the business at hand, asking their views of American life. The students rose when recognized and stood at attention, rattling off opinions with machine-gun speed but in perfectly formed sentences. "America is a great and powerful nation, and for that reason it is important for us to know about it," one student said and then sat down as briskly as she had arisen. "Americans are capable of great deeds, putting a man on the moon, for example," intoned another in the front row. "We respect them for that." Of course that has been the Russian classroom style for centuries: speak to the point, give the questioner what he wants to hear. But the students seemed constrained even beyond this norm. Their remarks suggested incantations passed down from generation to generation, with little attention to their substance. It didn't help that the principal kept intervening, reshaping my questions into her own terms. Some of the students looked in her direction rather than mine when answering. She was the angry god their words were meant to appease.

Frustrated, I shifted the ground a bit, suggesting that the students put a question to me for every one I asked them. It would make our encounter more balanced, an opinion for an opinion, a revelation for a revelation, and perhaps, I told myself, it would also short-circuit the principal's influence. But it didn't work out. "Could you tell us, please, the role the American Communist party now plays in the politics of your country?" "What about health care? Isn't it true that it is too expensive for the average American citizen?" The principal nodded in affirmation at each question, clearly proud that her charges were sticking to the prescribed issues. We were adrift in the horse latitudes of stereotypes, with the heavy skies of preconceptions pressing down.

When I recognized the next student, I no longer expected anything of interest to come of my visit. With an exaggerated air of importance, as if he were an orator addressing multitudes, a curly-haired boy with a merry air about him rose from his seat. He was greeted with a few giggles, which he mockingly acknowledged. "What about Texas?" he asked me. "How do they live there?"

I paused, uncertain what was meant. Struggling to contain his own giggling, the boy said, "You know. Cowboys and Indians, six-guns." He mimicked a gunfighter in action.

The classroom erupted in laughter. Some of the students hooted at the speaker, others turned to their neighbors to explain and repeat the gunfighting gesture. The principal tried to quell the storm but could not. The scene was completely unexpected, out of context, as if some wind of disorder had blown in the window and touched all of the students simultaneously. Still standing, enjoying the effect he had produced, the curly-haired boy was arguing with one of his hooting critics. He was talking extremely fast, using a lot of school slang, and I missed some of what he said. "Could you speak a bit slower?" I shouted in his direction. "I didn't catch all your words."

"Don't worry," said a student in the front row, "we can catch his words all right, and we still have no idea what he is talking about."

It was the first unaffected comment addressed to me since I had come to the school, and I took it as a sign that I was included in the shift of mood that had overtaken the class. It seemed a moment of sincere affection—not personal, which after all I had hardly earned, but affection for the country I willy-nilly represented.

I turned with anticipation to the next questioner. A large-boned blond girl, smoothing her uniform back into perfection as she came to attention, addressed me in the combative tones of a commissar.

She spoke in a rush, as if she had been waiting the whole time for an appropriate opening. "About World War II. Could you tell us why did Rockefeller sell engines to the Germans that the fascists could put into the tanks used to invade the Soviet Union?"

The charge is not new, having served as boilerplate for Soviet propagandists throughout the Cold War. I had heard versions in America too. I prepared to answer, though it had been put to me less as a question than an indictment. But, then, before I could speak, the principal intervened. She directed the blond girl, who had sat smugly down, to rise again. Moving to the center of the classroom and casually preempting the place where I had stood, she proceeded to deliver a little lecture on the protocol of questioning a visiting speaker. There is freedom of inquiry, of course, the new educational policies guarantee that; but the freedom must not extend to rudeness. The lecture went on for three or four minutes, during which time the blond girl stood motionless in the aisle. If she was humiliated by the shower of criticism, she gave no sign. Presumably it was established practice.

By the time the little lecture was over, any answer I might have made to the girl's question was beside the point. Indeed, though the discussion went on a bit longer, it wandered aimlessly. Whatever the intent, the disquisition on classroom etiquette had pushed the theme of America irretrievably into the background. To conclude the occasion, the principal presented me with a book with pictures from the Hermitage exhibit and, as is the custom, a bouquet of flowers, and the students applauded politely.

At first, I was sorry at the way the meeting with the class had turned so abruptly away from that moment when we had all happily contemplated the idea of Texas cowboys—it had been exhilarating. But, thinking about it, I realized that my regrets were probably misplaced. After all, Russians have often shown bursts of affection for America and Americans; the trick is to sustain these over time, expand the moment into a durable attitude. The principal must have been pleased with the way the afternoon had gone, the shortest of detours through a patch of untrammeled expression, to show it could be done if necessary, and then a brisk return to the beaten path.

Afterward, when all the students had left the classroom, she suggested we walk together to the metro stop several blocks away. Outside, it had started to rain lightly and she offered to share her umbrella, but I declined. I was juggling my briefcase and the gifts the class had given me, and besides the principal was quite short— we would have jostled and tripped over each other and both ended up wet. We talked about the weather and Moscow's inadequate sewers and she told me where to find the best bakery in town, down on Gorky Street. We did not talk about my chat with the students or about Russian-American relations.

But at the entrance to the metro, as we were about to part, she said, "You know, I am a Muscovite, born and raised here. I was in Moscow during the Great War when there were Americans around. I met several of them because my father was an administrator in the Lend-Lease Program. I remember liking them. Americans are a friendly people."

It was clear that she had offered her reminiscence as some sort of extraordinary concession. She wanted—indeed, from the look in her eye, I would say that she demanded—some reciprocating gesture. I had not liked her meddling in the classroom, and in general found her officious manner not to my taste, but I was grateful that she had allowed me into her school at all. A few years ago, such a visit would have been impossible, and it still had taken some courage on her part. The risk to me had of course been nil, which put me all the more in her debt.

Standing in the rain amidst the rush-hour crowds, I could not find a response that would properly cap the encounter. It suddenly seemed more complex than I had thought. So, instead, I simply thrust the bouquet of flowers that I was carrying into her hand. Her stern features rearranged themselves into a smile, and she was still smiling when she walked away from me to her bus stop. It was, I suppose, a conventional accord that we had reached, lacking all genuine feeling. But that's the best that was available.

Given the intervening name-calling and squabbling, it is sometimes hard to recall that progressive-minded Russians of the nineteenth century—including those who were the precursors of the
Bolsheviks—admired America's political institutions. Nikolai
Chernyshevsky, the soul of the radical movement, announced that
all those who criticized the United States were in effect endorsing
the status quo everywhere, while those who admired it were in
favor of "reforming existing relations," including, by inescapable
implication, the relations promoted by the hated tsarist regime.

America seemed a laboratory where marvelous social experiments were being conducted. The hope was that forms created
there also could be utilized in the land of the Romanovs. For some
Russians, indeed, it was only a short jump to the next logical stage:
Why wait for reported results, when it was possible to come to the
laboratory and conduct the experiment personally? A number of
Russians (including Nikolai Chaikovsky, a key figure in the radical
movement) made the trip, and many more planned to. Students at
Kiev University, for example, formed an "American Circle" to
discuss emigration. One notable sign of the Russian faith in America's political life was the Progressive Commune, which was established in Cedarvale, Kansas, in 1871. The guiding spirit was
Vladimir Geins, son of a major general of the Imperial Army on
the verge of a brilliant career in the Surveying Corps when he
decided that only America could contain his utopian dreams. His
wife followed with alacrity—she would, she announced, rather be
the wife of a poor American farmer than of a Russian general.
Russia implied stagnation, whereas in America a proper social life
could still be invented.

Their experience in America put their ideals to a severe test.
After briefly participating in a furniture cooperative shop in Brook-
lyn, Geins and his wife moved on to Missouri, attracted by advertisements in the magazine *The Communist*. In the town of
Minersville, they joined the Reunion Community. It consisted of
fifteen adults and ten children huddled together in a small house
and was led by a "hygienic physician" who advocated improvement

through hydropathy. After staying a short time and finding themselves on the edge of poverty, the Geinses made their way to the Osage Trust Lands in southern Kansas, which the government had just opened for settlement. Joined by several like-minded Russians, they established the Progressive Commune. The guiding motto was "From each according to his ability, to each according to his wants," but socialist ideology was mixed with makeshift principles, including vegetarianism, prohibition of tobacco and alcohol, and weekly meetings devoted to mutual criticism—a forerunner of the *samokritik* sessions that became notorious in the early years of the Soviet Union. There were immense practical difficulties. Membership never exceeded eleven adults, none of whom had any experience at farming. Living conditions soon slipped to a subsistence level. One menu, not atypical, sounds like a bad joke: corn gruel and graham bread for breakfast and graham gruel and corn bread for dinner. There was continuous squabbling about the division of chores and several flare-ups when lovers changed partners. One of the members described the mutual-criticism meetings, which at first had seemed proof of a visionary harmony, as sessions of "mutual irritation."

The Progressive Commune dissolved in 1879, a dismal failure, but, remarkably, the belief guiding its creation was largely unshaken. To most of the communards, America remained a congenial place for men of a progressive stamp. Sustaining evidence ranged from the fact that it had been possible to set up a working commune at all (the U.S. government provided 160 acres at $1.25 an acre, no questions asked about political orientation) to the memorable friendliness of neighbors. Most compelling of all were America's political institutions, even in the rough form encountered on the frontier. On the way to join the commune, one Russian accidentally shot his traveling companion and was placed under arrest by the local sheriff, a bearded harness-maker still wearing his leather apron. In jail, the Russian assumed the proceedings would follow the tsarist model, and resigned himself to a long wait for trial, then certain conviction; but the trial took place within an hour, was conducted with scrupulous if informal fairness, and concluded in an acquittal on all charges.

"All my life in America," Geins remarked in later years, I endured the direst physical privations, and my social activity resulted in the cruelest disappointments. But then I experienced the loftiest joys of which man is capable . . . I left America with a feeling of deep gratitude for its political institutions, its upright, energetic public men, for its multitude of people. . . ." Geins's endorsement of America over and above all its flaws was representative of Russian progressive opinion. Even the harshest criticism—and slavery was severely censured—did not dim the fervid curiosity, bordering on awe, with which American political life was regarded. When the poet Alexander Pushkin remarked that American life "was darkened by a very dark shadow" of racism, he added that what the shadow fell across was "an admirable political organization, which surpasses all that mankind could have had and even dreamed of since the creation of the world." Pushkin was famous for his unblinking, direct style; America moved him to hyperbole.

I was curious to see how the reputation of American political life was faring. A Russian friend, thinking it might be relevant, suggested I see the dramatic ballet *Stars and Death*. The title sounded both tendentious and humorless, but there were balancing factors— the show was at the Taganka Theater, which has long had a liberal outlook, it came recommended by a friend who was earnestly pro-American, and this was, after all, Gorbachevian Russia, land of comity and goodwill toward all nations. I decided that in sum the auguries for an interesting depiction of America looked favorable. I was wrong. I endured an evening of agit-prop anti-Americanism of a kind I thought had gone out with the Cold War.

The plot concerns a group of Chileans who leave their happy but impoverished land in the 1850s to seek riches in California, only to end up as exploited stoop laborers. Not content with making the American masters appear Simon-Legree cruel, *Stars and*

*Death* makes them barbarously boorish as well. When not oppressing Chileans, they spend their time at lewd burlesques or throwing food at each other while singing idiotic ditties. No matter what one thinks of nineteenth-century California labor practices, the show's effect was like getting hit on the head for a few hours, and I left the theater feeling I had been assaulted. For the rest of the evening one of the ditties, "How do you do, Mr. Jones?," kept coming to mind, each time making me want to scream—not about capitalism's corruption but about socialism's inept propaganda.

In fact, gloating, nasty-minded attacks on America are a disappearing genre in the Soviet theater. What I had seen was probably a reflex twitching as the Soviet body politic shifted into a new posture. But if that explains the production of the ballet itself, it does not account for the response of my friend when I told her what I thought of *Stars and Death.*

"It was a bit self-righteous, don't you think?" I said.

"Why? It seemed *normalno,*" Vera replied, using the catchword that indicates a condition completely devoid of surprises.

Vera likes Americans, half believing we are the designated saviors of the world, and yet she saw nothing remarkable in a spectacle that damned our country's political life as ruthless and exploitative. It was not the gist of her opinion that unsettled me—I didn't have to travel to Moscow to be persuaded the position had merit—but the blandness with which it was stated. She was like a distracted hanging judge, uninterested in the condemned man's background and ummoved by his promises to be good.

We were sitting in her cramped kitchen, which was no bigger than a closet, drinking tea with jam and feeling content that we were inside while a wind-driven rain beat on the windows. I had met Vera only a week before, but already I felt at home. Friendship in Russia can spark to life very fast. She told me her life story—a narrative that moved from the high point of a brief marriage to a fellow archaeology student down to this small apartment in a dreary Moscow outskirt, which she shared with her young daughter. The plot was not happy, but Vera related it with a bracing irony that kept me laughing. I thought I knew her. But now, looking at her perched on a stool wedged against a whining old refrigerator, I felt a chasm of misunderstanding opening up. The cool complacency of that *normalno* threw me off balance.

Vera was not exceptional. Even among well-educated Russians, opinions of our domestic politics are less of an intellectual position than a habit of mind. They may speak knowledgeably about our material wealth or our cultural spectacle or our foreign policies, but America's daily political life somehow eludes them completely. It makes for disorienting encounters. I have sat through the night with friends drinking vodka and resolving questions about the meaning of existence, and then suddenly felt all common ground give way when the discussion turned to the feminist movement. (For most Russians, that issue is still only an occasion for snide jokes about bras.) Can there be fascination without curiosity, interest without knowledge? At least as regards our domestic politics, Russians seem to have achieved this singular condition.

It seems a bit like what psychiatrists call a reactive formation, the scary stimulus in this case being Soviet propaganda. The early Bolsheviks were intent on obliterating all traces of the nineteenth-century admiration for American political life, and the nastiness directed our way in pre-Gorbachev times—cartoons, for example, commonly depicted American politicians as jackbooted fascists with blood dripping from their jaws or a marauding KKK mob—had the teeth-gnashing, foaming fury of exorcism. It was not unreasonable for citizens to respond to this ferocity with pointed indifference, like a bystander sidling out of the way of a street brawl. Why get involved in somebody else's fight? Politics in revolutionary Russia was the possession of the state, and American politics touched most citizens even less. The posture was one that could easily become a habit, and even now, when the official line on America has become milder, there is little inclination among most Russians to think very deeply about our feminist movement or our forms of local government or our labor unions—the whole hurly-burly that makes up our domestic scene. As regards that, *normalno* will do just fine.

One constant target of the propaganda machine has been American racism. Over the years, the Soviet Union has kept up a drumbeat of self-congratulatory concern. Lenin put "The Negro Question" on the agenda of the 1920 Comintern meeting, and it immediately began to figure prominently in Soviet ideology, attracting extensive coverage in academic and political publications and in the popular press. But all the excited commentary seems to have produced little knowledge. Arriving in Moscow in 1932 to serve as consultant for a Soviet film about American blacks, the poet Langston Hughes was astounded by the working script. "It was written by a famous Russian author who had never been in America. . . . From [a few books] he had put together what he thought was a highly dramatic story of labor and race relations in the United States. But the end result was a script improbable to the point of ludicrousness." All of Hughes's suggested changes were brushed aside as irrelevant. The 1920s and early 1930s were a time when numerous American blacks traveled to the Soviet Union, to see if socialism lived up to its promises to offer a better life; but meeting American blacks seems to have little influenced the picture Soviets had already formulated. In one case Soviet officials who greeted a visiting delegation of American blacks refused to let a light-skinned member act as the group's leader, deeming him unrepresentative of the race.

It does not take a very long stay in the Soviet Union to see that not much has changed since those days. Black America remains terra incognita to most Russians. The events that began with the civil rights movement and which have altered the American scene might as well never have happened. Cultural achievements (except for jazz) are dismissed, economic gains overlooked, new educational opportunities discounted. There is of course an argument to be made that the conditions of blacks have really not improved, but Russians do not make an argument; their opinions have the exasperating air of oracle. A few years ago, *Krokodil,* the biweekly journal of humor, printed a cartoon showing the Statue of Liberty from two perspectives—at a distance she seems a shimmering symbol of democracy, but in close-up her crown proves to be decorated with Ku Klux Klansmen armed with knouts and pistols. This still says all that most Soviets know or want to know about the status of blacks in America: lynch law prevails, and oppression has reached barbaric levels. It's worth adding that not a few Russians think this excellent policy—every second taxi driver congratulated me on living in a country that keeps blacks in their place, usually adding some nasty advice about what should be done to white women who consort with black men. A white American in Moscow is reduced to playing one of two roles: despised agent of an evil oppressor or admired agent of a system that keeps the uppity in their place.

I find it best, when in Russia, to steer clear of the matter altogether, and it was only an acute curiosity that made me attend a recital of gospel songs by the black American Joe Carter. I wanted to see how a full-blown, we-know-the-truth, propaganda spectacle was performed in the Age of Gorbachev, and this seemed just the right ticket. The recital was in one of the prestigious halls off Karl Marx Square. The audience consisted mainly of official youth groups enduring their prescribed recreation. The man who introduced Carter reached for extravagant terms, as if he had been consulting a Leninist thesaurus. The decks were cleared for a presentation of American blacks as Soviet society would have them. The Soviets have been doing this sort of propaganda spectacle for so long that they have become very proficient, every stop in place, every meaning underscored.

Carter, tall and full-bearded and so broad through the chest that his tuxedo hardly contained him, was imposing, and left to his own devices he probably would have given a lively performance; as it was, he was hemmed in by a translator who preceded each song with a lugubrious explanation about the sorry history of black

Americans. Carter was reduced to a stick figure representing the minorities that capitalism grinds down. His thundering voice, especially as the audience didn't know English, was only the plangent cry of a man with no future. Even if one believes in the moral of the story, there was something mind-numbing in its telling.

During intermission, I wandered through the crowd milling around the refreshment stands. No one was complaining that the propaganda was too shrill. On the other hand, no one was remarking on how much they were enjoying the performance. For most of the spectators, young people already in the Party or destined for membership shortly, it was just another day at the office. I asked one young girl what she thought.

"*Normalno,*" she replied, hardly looking up.

I considered leaving without watching the second half of the recital, but finally decided to stay. To tell the truth, a sort of gloating curiosity had gotten the better of me—it was fascinating to watch how the Russians' loudly proclaimed sympathy for American blacks dissolved into inept posturing right before my eyes.

I was glad I stayed. At the end there was an unexpected moment. After Carter finished the last number, five young girls carrying flowers crossed the stage and approached him. He accepted the bouquets with formal dignity. Then, as the last girl presented her gift and was about to turn away, he took her by the elbow and bent forward to kiss her on the cheek. The girl froze, clearly wanting to move away but held still by politeness. When Carter's lips touched her cheek, no more than the slightest brushing really, there was a palpable intake of breath from the audience. The woman sitting next to me clucked as she shook her head disapprovingly.

It was not, I think, black and white skin touching that sent a *frisson* of shock through the audience (though, given the law of averages, there would certainly have been some bigots in a Russian gathering of that size). Rather, it was that the occasion, so predictable till this point, had taken an unexpected turn; it was a problem of scripting as much as of race relations. Carter had been cast as a representative figure, and the kiss was not part of his role. Perhaps he meant to puncture the smothering pomp of the occasion, or perhaps he was possessed by a gracious whim; in any case, for a moment, Carter had escaped the straitjacket of the propaganda spectacle.

The audience sat silent for a few seconds, uncertain what to make of Carter's gesture. Perhaps some among them were beginning to wonder what exactly they were doing in this darkened hall on such a fine fall afternoon. But then the man who had introduced Carter at the beginning of the recital stepped forward and began to applaud with huge movements of his arms, as if he were beating a big pillow. The audience picked up the cue, and soon everyone in the hall was clapping in the rhythmic style Russians favor. The program moved smoothly to its conclusion. Carter's kiss was forgiven or acclaimed or forgotten—in the noisy hubbub of the spectacle, it was impossible to know which.

As the audience spilled out of the hall, I found myself moved along by a group of jostling teenagers. They were, I gathered, members of a youth group scheduled for a soccer match later that day, and they were boisterous with expectation. When they spotted a few members of the group that was their prospective opponent, there were a lot of playful taunts and catcalls. Just kids having a good time, like anywhere else in the world, but their giddiness was made striking by being so at odds with their by-the-numbers behavior during the recital.

I was seeing, I realized, an essential bit of Russian sociology. This country is filled end to end with groups—not only youth groups, but workers' clubs, neighborhood cells, pensioners' associations, all of them founded by an appeal to one Leninist principle or another. It is through these groups that Russians find their recreation, or companionship on dull winter evenings, or even how they manage such practical matters as securing tickets to the ballet or reserving a tennis court. That is the real function of Soviet ideology today, not as a body of compelling ideas, but as an aspect of social organization, and until some other justification for these groups comes along, ideology will have a role in this country, and with it those traditional propaganda spectacles. Indeed, though many Russians are fed up with hoary Leninist doctrines and slogans, their protests are muted. Spending an afternoon listening to denunciations of American racism, for example, may seem a fair trade-off for the pleasures of well-organized soccer competitions.

## two

# Dreams
# of
# Capitalism

**M**oscow stores and restaurants and all the various bureaus pride themselves on the number of ways they can say "closed"—closed for inventory, closed for renovation, service for special groups only, sanitation day. It's true art-for-art's sake embroidery, since all the terms really have a single meaning, something on the order of "gone fishing." I waited with a dozen others in front of a produce store with a sign proclaiming it would reopen when inventory-taking would be completed. Twenty minutes after the appointed time, exasperated, we burst through the door to find the five shopgirls at ease in one corner, having a smoke and a chat. They got to their feet slowly, with no apologies, annoyed at the interruption. Slackers in the Soviet Union are slackers with a real dedication to their calling. I would not have been surprised to hear that the city zoo was closed because the beasts had decided to shed their official animality for a while, reclining in bare slothfulness instead.

What you get here is not mere disorganization but rather chaos bulging through a tattered network of innumerable rules and conventions. Stores don't only slam their doors in the face of customers; they offer highfalutin excuses everyone knows are empty. Desk clerks haughtily announce that the hotel's high standards require that you surrender your room key each time you leave; when you return, they let you cool your heels for ten minutes while they finish their personal telephone calls. Doormen block entry to restaurants by saying they fear overcrowding the premises; but they turn away clients even when three-quarters of the tables are unoccupied. The social structure presents itself as a finely tuned machine, but the gears grind at every turn.

One afternoon I joined a queue that had formed on a street corner near a makeshift counter unexpectedly selling fresh grapes. I was about thirtieth in line. People in front and behind kept leaving to check the progress of another queue down the street, towing a friend or two back with them when they returned to reclaim their places. One man, waving some documents, simply broke in at the head of the line. I looked inquiringly at the fellow next to me. "Invalided war veteran," he said. "Special privileges." A woman, waving her documents, also moved directly to the head of the line. "*Mnogodetnaya mat,*" my neighbor said, using the bureaucratic term for a mother with three or more children. "Special privileges," he added with a weary shrug. So it went. After twenty minutes I was no closer to the counter, though it seemed that a whole new set of people now stood between me and my goal. I could see the supply of grapes vanishing, as in one of those cotton-wadded dreams where the prize is always tantalizingly out of reach. But there was no point in complaining. This was the Soviet way of doing things.

Russians are well aware of these problems, complaints about stores and services being the main topic of casual conversations. Few expect improvement any time soon, things having been too long in their present rut, but what hopes do exist often are cast in the form of an American model. Of all areas of life, this is the one where the American aura shines brightest. Our recent economic difficulties, which have lowered America's stock in much of the world, have made little impression here. Russians still believe fervently that America's economy is not only the most provident but the most efficient.

This faith, indeed, has something of the status of myth, and as with any myth, dating the origin is difficult. There is one valuable bit of linguistic evidence. The Russian word for "steamboat" is *parakhod,* but *stimbot* had some currency at the beginning of the nineteenth century. Russians of the time apparently thought of the vessels as particularly American, and hence best denominated by some fractured rendering of American speech. Pavel Svinin, who as a Russian diplomat in Philadelphia witnessed the voyages of Robert Fulton's *Paragon* on the Hudson River, wrote, "Conceive of a vessel having the appearance of a flat-bottomed frigate; imagine it to be unafraid of storms, independent of the wind, careless of foul weather, to move with amazing speed and security, and to run on scheduled time; while inside are peace and tranquillity, and the very whims of luxury; such is the American steamboat [*amerikanskiy stimbot*]." Not, significantly, a steamboat built in America or by an American, but "the American steamboat"—to Svinin and his contemporaries the adjective and noun fit together naturally.

The steamboat was an instance of American engineering dexterity, but it was not that alone that held Russians' attention. Svinin's references to the *Paragon*'s luxurious interiors and its adherence to schedules indicate an admiration for more than technology. Svinin, who was an artist of some talent, made a drawing of the *Paragon* under way: he depicted the passengers at ease on the open deck, drinking beer, smoking, even trolling for fish as the boat made its way up the Hudson. It is a picture of transportation as recreation. The point of American technology was social convenience; to anyone who had to endure the chaos of Russian everyday life, that principle had an almost religious allure.

Svinin hoped Fulton's invention could be introduced into Russia, and the Hudson Navigational Company did in fact petition for a charter granting monopolistic rights. In the petition Fulton indicated his plan to begin "steamboat communication between St. Petersburg and Kronshtadt [*sic*]," thus allowing the nobility easy passage between the capital and their country estates. Svinin had something grander in mind. In his vision the steamboat would not only carry people from place to place but would be the focal point of a new, better-ordered society. "With pleasure do I imagine the advantages that will flow from the introduction of steamboats into Russia. . . . Joy, conjugal life and fidelity will establish themselves in the once abandoned villages, and the peasants who suffered exhaustion and sometimes death from barge-towing will find true riches and health behind the plow." As it happened, Fulton was unable to realize in Russia either the practical or the visionary implications of his invention. Negotiations, already bogged down in the swamps of the imperial bureaucracy, foundered for good when the War of 1812 hindered communication. As a gesture of goodwill (and to advance his petition), Fulton named the last steamboat he built *The Emperor of Russia,* but at his death in 1815 the monopoly charter had still not been secured. (The Ministry of Internal Affairs ultimately decided to foster a native steamboat industry instead.) Although Fulton's *stimbot* never made it to Russia, the ideal of American efficiency did. America has set the standard for making everyday life comfortable and well-organized for almost two centuries.

Russians who come to America are often most impressed by our little conveniences. Even when they dismiss our grander accomplishments, they are brought up short by all those devices and designs that make America tidy and well-run. Who would have thought to do this here and to put that there? Not a Russian, apparently. When Alexander Lakier recorded his impressions of his 1861 trip around America in his book *Journey Through the North American States, Canada and Cuba,* he devoted three pages to the marvels of a Boston hotel, rhapsodizing over everything from the check-in procedures to the speaking tubes that let the manager communicate with the maids on the higher floors. "The organization is a model of simplicity and attentiveness," Lakier declared, no doubt made wistful by memories of the doss houses of Imperial Russia. Seventy years later, it was American laundries that captivated Ilf and Petrov. "Each one of [the shirts] is placed in a paper packet, around which is a paper ribbon with the trade-mark of laundry." Providing clean shirts promptly was beyond the capacity of the Soviet economy, but at least it was an understandable procedure; placing a ribbon on the wrapping was a gesture that almost defied conceptualization. No reason for the practice existed except the desire to make things look a bit tidier. America seems a marvel—not merely technologically adept but technologically extravagant, always pressing efficiency forward an extra degree. That is the point, indeed, of a joke that circulated in Russia for a while about the Chicago slaughterhouses. The process, it was said, had come to such a point that a pig could be put into one end of a machine and have it come out at the other as a salami—and if the salami was not satisfactory, putting the machine in reverse would once more produce a live pig.

Russians often speak of how nice it would be to transplant American efficiency to their native land, but between the idea and the reality falls the shadow of tradition. Russians have done things one way so long that they cannot imagine doing otherwise. It's not surprising that America's little efficiencies can strike them as miraculous, simultaneously simple and yet impossible to copy. They try, but they most often resemble someone put to work on a jigsaw puzzle without being shown the completed image, expending furious energy on details without ever approaching a larger success.

Consider the reaction of Anastas Mikoyan (at the time the minister in charge of the Soviet Union's food industries) to a simple hamburger stand that he saw while on a visit to the United States. Mikoyan's description sounds knowing, but it is possible to detect a note of desperation. "A stainless steel plate is heated by gas or electricity. All this is built into a unit that is somewhat larger than a stall, so that it is possible to stand and work it in the street. The clerk puts the meat on this plate without any fat, for the 'hamburger' has itself enough fat, thereby precluding the necessity for the addition of this substance. The patty is cooked on one side, then on the other—and it is ready in a couple of minutes. The clerk has a bun for the patty. He cuts the roll, puts in the patty, adds ketchup, a slice of pickle, or mustard, and there it is—a sandwich ready to eat." This is a classic statement of the Soviet predicament vis-à-vis the United States. The obsessive detail is testimony to a sensibility that can admire a phenomenon but cannot conceive of how to duplicate it. The American hamburger stand is no less mysterious than a sorcerer at work, and the only way to comprehend the hocus-pocus is through a plodding recitation of each of the physical movements.

Mikoyan made his trip in 1936, but his report, with its exhortatory description of hamburger stands, was first published in 1971, which fact accurately suggests that Russia's food service had not progressed very far in thirty-five years. Even today there are only a handful of outdoor food stands, none of them up to the standard Mikoyan had seen in New York a half-century ago. I several times tried to have a snack at the stand outside the Hotel Intourist, but each time gave up as the line inched forward at turtle pace. Each cup of coffee had to be brewed separately, no matter what the cost in waiting time; each portion of ice cream had to be weighed out to the gram. At first glance, the place looked like any New York City fast-food stand, but though the elements were similar, some final tap to get them into proper alignment had been overlooked.

Social efficiency is basic to communist theory—a god-term much in the same manner as "the pursuit of happiness" has been for us. The early Bolsheviks extolled the perfectly rationalized Soviet society of the near future while snickering at the disorderliness of capitalistic economies. Communism would not only provide, it would do so neatly; the West would sink beneath the double burden of inequity and sloppiness. But social efficiency has been most visible as a capitalist practice—an incidental result of the deplorable drive to maximize profit, but nonetheless real. This unexpected development forced an intellectual balancing act on Soviet officials; though often invoking the West (and most often America) as an economic model, they had to be careful not to offend political dogma. Stalin suggested the standard in a speech in 1924. "We must mix American practicality with Bolshevik ideology," he announced, and left to others, often at the peril of their lives, the job of figuring out exactly how these abstract categories were to be applied in practice.

Today's conditions require an adjustment in Stalin's formula, Bolshevik ideology having largely fallen by the wayside. But the basic idea of blending America and Russia is alive and well. The most vivid example of such cooperation is the joint venture— American companies and Soviet official and quasi-official individuals and agencies going into business together, sharing the profits and risks from enterprises that produce everything from computer software to pizza.

One active promoter of these ventures is Sergei Goryachev, director of the Executive Board of the Moscow region, a position which might be described as the equivalent of a New York City borough president without the ribbon-cutting ceremonies. His office was on Kropotkin Street, in what once had been the home of P. A. Vyazemsky, a participant in the unsuccessful 1825 rebellion against Nicholas I known as the Decembrist Uprising. Like most of the Decembrists, Vyazemsky belonged to the upper nobility, and his house showed it. It had the sweep and classical elegance of a small palace; broad stairs led to the second floor, where once high society met for dances and witty conversations and where now bureaucrats sit in at meetings and write reports. I waited in an antechamber for ten minutes, then was shown in to a Mussolini-type office, a large room with a monumental desk at one end that seemed designed to cow the entering petitioner. But Goryachev was no Mussolini. He was very affable, with an unstoppable sort of optimism. More than Mussolini, he suggested the head of a chamber of commerce in one of our Midwestern states.

A McDonald's on Pushkin Square was very exciting, he said in answer to my question. Yes, he had heard the criticism that fast-food outlets generate a lot of refuse, but that only meant more attention should be paid to garbage collection. No doubt neighborhood residents would still complain, but that could not be helped. "When we decide to put a fish store somewhere, neighborhood residents object to the smell. When we decide to put a factory somewhere, neighborhood residents object to the noise. Now they will object to the garbage. There is no answer," he said, speaking in the tones of a man who has long ago stopped contemplating the socialist ideal of a perfect concordance of interests.

One of Goryachev's current projects was a joint American-Soviet venture to build a new restaurant. It will be called "The Trenton," in honor of the American partner's hometown; in the Soviet Union that presumably evokes an image as exotic and lovely as "Tour d'Argent" or "Maxim's." There would be, Goryachev told me, a special menu for tourists, but the main trade would be Russians.

"We still have to figure out a way to get a quicker turnover of customers. Russian people, when they go to a restaurant, they plan to spend the whole night sitting at the table, five hours or so." He presented it as a problem that would be soon solved; everything was possible, and all was for the best in this best of all possible worlds.

As our discussion began to wind down, I remarked on the marvelous Vyazemsky manor. By way of an answer, he flicked on the intercom and summoned an assistant, who was in the room in thirty seconds. "Our visitor is interested in the history of our building," he said, leaning back in his chair and folding his hands behind his head in the ostentatious pose of an interested listener. The assistant, a schoolmarmish woman in her forties, launched into a little lecture on the architectural niceties of the different rooms and the exterior, digressing briefly to explain the political significance of the Decembrist Uprising. Throughout Goryachev smiled vaguely and nodded; he seemed detached yet still supervisory. I had the feeling that this little detour into high culture was only an oblique extension of the commercial plans he had laid out for me earlier—as American corporations invoke beautiful beaches to sell deodorant, so here the pitch was history. The newly enterprising Soviet economy was looking forward to a profitable future while resting on an eventful past.

When the assistant's presentation was over, Goryachev walked out with me to the front entrance. He asked if I'd like to borrow his chauffeur-driven car for a while; he knew Moscow's transportation system could be tiring for someone with several appointments in one day. He seemed suddenly relaxed, more sincere, as if the rigmarole of commerce had been an ill-fitting coat he had discarded once formalities were over. As we said good-bye, he wiped some sweat from his upper lip; the effort of fitting into the mold of an American entrepreneur can be taxing.

Outside again, I noticed that directly across the street was the Leo Tolstoy Museum, housed in the great man's one-time Moscow residence. I thought I'd have a look inside, perhaps touch the desk where *Resurrection* had been written. But I found the front door locked. Through the glass I saw a woman leaning on a mop and scolding a man who sat on a stool with a glazed look on his face. She came in response to my knock, opened the door a crack, and barked at me, "Sanitation day."

"But there is no sign," I remonstrated.

"Sanitation day," she repeated, slamming the door with evident pleasure and going back to her scolding.

The juxtaposition was delicious: on the one hand, Goryachev's grand commercial plans; on the other, Russia's traditional public-be-damned attitude. I pictured The Trenton in operation, patrons being moved briskly through their meals by modern psychological tricks while at the entrance a grumpy doorman imperiously turned away all comers.

The need for better services is so blatant in Russia that there can seem to be no choice: it is necessary to find the policies and programs that will promote change. But economics is always also social psychology, and this makes the issue less clear cut. The slow pace Russians prefer, their taciturn rejection of the idea that the customer is always right—these traits have a reverse side that can be very endearing. I often find it hard to resist those cashiers in cafeterias who won't provide change until they pronounce on all the details of a proper diet or taxi drivers who take roundabout routes so they can finish their argument proving that God exists. There is a pleasant Old World rhythm here, far from America's exhausting tempo. Still, a lot depends on the particular circumstances. Standing on one of those interminable queues, it's hard not to believe that a country that makes you wait twenty minutes for a cup of coffee has failed to meet some minimum requirement of civilization. In fact, daily life here is irritating and genial in about equal measure, and judgment of it can waver crazily. Russia's dubious accomplishment is to have made modernity seem problematic.

Seryozha is one of the most Americanized Russians I met. He was always dapper, his favorite outfit a tan suit, tan shoes, white socks. He was in his early forties, and trim; I noticed that he kept a set of barbells in his bedroom. His thin-framed glasses—of American design, I would bet—sat neatly on his sharp nose. He spoke perfect, colloquial English. He could pass for a Hollywood dealmaker, which I believe was what he wished to be.

He worked in Dom Kino on Kiev Street, the home of the filmmakers union, where he was involved in several joint Soviet-American projects. The union was one of the first Soviet organizations to support Gorbachev's call for more open relations with the West, so it got in on the ground floor when praxis followed theory and some deals were struck. But Seryozha's ideas sometimes seemed too visionary to stay within any organizational confines. He outlined his complicated plans to me while maneuvering his Fiat aggressively through rush-hour traffic. Excited by his own comments, Seryozha kept turning toward me to see if I got the gist. Our reckless progress along Kutuzovsky Prospect—the other cars changed lanes as randomly and with as little warning as we did—seemed somehow to prod his commercial enthusiasm, and as he spoke of enticing foreign investors, coping with currency restrictions, devising surveys, his tone became constrained, almost strangulated in a manner that suggested ideas multiplying too fast for words to keep up. He seemed overwhelmed and challenged simultaneously. Was this the way it was in turn-of-the-century America, when capitalism was still a vivid, unsullied dream?

In the kitchen of his apartment, on top of the built-in wooden cabinets, there was a long row of perhaps a hundred empty liquor bottles with English and French and Italian labels, souvenirs of some grand evenings, he told me. I drank cup after cup of tea and ate spice cookies and listened to a discussion between Seryozha and a prominent Moscow film director. The homey setting belied the grandiosity of the topic, which was no less than how to start a new movie company, something on the model of a Hollywood studio.

Money was no object. The director had plenty at his disposal. Many Soviet institutions, such as trade unions or retail stores, accumulate considerable sums; rather than give this over to the state in taxes, they support cultural activities, a movie studio being an option no worse than others. But even after this was explained to me, it was disorienting to see something so grand being conceived around an ordinary kitchen table.

Seryozha fairly bubbled with ideas. To get scripts, they would advertise. Those submitted would be turned over to a committee of critics who would recommend changes, which would be incorporated by members of the studio's writers' stable. A rough version of the completed film would be shown to selected audiences; their reaction, as recorded on questionnaires, could lead to more changes.

To me it sounded like Hollywood at its worst. "But what about artistic integrity?" I asked. "Doesn't that count for something?"

Seryozha glanced sharply at me, presumably surprised by an American who didn't understand American ways, and then returned to his conversation with the director. "We'll send out reviews to newspapers in all the major cities," he declared. "Not these long complicated articles our critics write now, but three paragraphs or so, the way they do it in America. The newspapers do not have to know that the reviewers are connected to the studio—the point is to give them information, allow them to grasp quickly the sort of film that is available."

The director agreed. The deal seemed to be going forward at a dizzying speed. After an hour, when I said I had to be going, the two of them were still in the deep waters of marketing strategies.

Escorting me out to the elevator, Seryozha became uncharacteristically pensive. Sighing deeply, he said, "It sometimes seems to me that I've been waiting years to do the sorts of things I am now finally doing."

These days, many Russians stroll around in doubt and confusion, but people like Seryozha are living on a fine edge of exhilaration. Many of them have profited financially, but that is not the main reason for joy. They have suddenly found that the world around them, which used to be only an irritant, can be made to conform to their inner urges. Watching Seryozha, I never saw a false step that might suggest he was learning a new role in life; he was, instead, coming to be himself for the first time. This gave him a kind of charm, the special grace of those unexpectedly discovering their inherent talents.

For a while I couldn't decide why Seryozha cared to spend time with me. Though gracious, he was often distracted. He had more important things to do than drink coffee and chat about the changing times. Then I hit upon an explanation. He wanted not my company but my presence; more precisely, he wanted the presence of an American. It gave his plans—his life—a fitting backdrop. I was someone who should be able to grasp his ideas with no more difficulty than breathing, whereas with Russians he had constantly to explain and qualify. I remembered the sharp, angry look he had given me when I had questioned his ideas about tailoring his films to popular taste; he must have felt like a trapeze artist who reaches out for the safety of his partner's grip only to find it is not there.

Seryozha was occasionally moody and he could be abrupt, but I never turned down his invitation. I wanted to be around to admire what seemed to me an almost metaphysical exploit on his part. Seryozha had tricked history. The pressure of economics has forced Russians into the role of America's students, looking to us for models of a well-run society. But as with many students, their relations with the teacher are ambivalent. Some are overly eager to emulate us, others shuffle off in determined opposition. But Seryozha was his own man. To him, America was less a teacher than a happy confirmation of what he knew on his own. Looking at him, I would think that here was the product to which Seryozha should apply his salesman skills—himself, his self-confidence, his go-getter urge. The market is potentially huge, the only problem being that many Russians are so far unaware that not having these qualities constitutes a lack.

If you take the metro to the Avtozavodskaya stop, then walk two blocks along Kuzhukhovsky Boulevard, past uninspiring shops and new but already decaying apartment-house blocks, you come to a remarkable structure. No plaque marks its significance; it seems no more than an ordinary automobile factory, smoky and grim. On the day I went, there was a fine drizzle that made it even more dreary. But the history of the building gives it a distinctiveness that virtually shines. In the 1930s, part of the plant's interior was laid out in accordance with Henry Ford's latest theories of mass production, with the hands-on help of Ford engineers and technicians. The plant, which nowadays turns out the ZIL car, commemorates that moment when a captain of American capitalism nurtured communism's infant industries. (Ford was paid, but his chief motive was the chance to disseminate his innovative labor practices, which he believed would save the world.) The Ford company figured even more prominently in the construction of other plants, most notably one in Nizhny Novgorod (now Gorky) that was designed by Albert Kahn, who was also the architect of the Ford plant in River Rouge, Michigan. When the first Gaz-A—the Russian equivalent of the Model A—rolled off the Nizhny Novgorod assembly line, the workers jubilantly toasted the American supervisors and blanket-tossed them into the air, the traditional way of showing affection. The event made front-page news in *Pravda*.

The Ford connection began in the 1920s. The intense antagonism that then existed between capitalism and communism, with each camp aggressively deriding the economic life of the other, suggests that these were bad times for commercial contact; in fact, Ford was only one of numerous American companies that did business with the Soviet Union in the 1920s and early 1930s. America pursued a schizophrenic course. The government remained aloof from a regime that came to power with a policy for confiscating private property, but corporate America lunged forward with arms open. The lure of new markets, especially as the Depression began to dry up the old ones, persuaded companies like General Electric, International Harvester, and Westinghouse to enter into trade agreements with the Soviets.

But it was Ford that was always in the forefront, not only in its share of the market but also as the brightest symbol of the American economy. Some Western visitors who toured the Russian countryside reported meeting peasants who could not identify Stalin but knew who Ford was. It was, after all, Ford's name that was inscribed on the tractor that was easing the daily routine of backbreaking labor. Postrevolutionary Russia was a country where the car and tractor were, if not kings, then pretenders to the throne whose ascension was eagerly awaited. Ford products flowed into Russia. Between 1920 and 1926, the Soviet government bought 25,000 Fordson trucks; by 1929, a full 85 percent of the trucks and tractors in the country were Ford-built, and many others were Ford copies, constructed (in violation of international patent law) in Leningrad and Moscow factories. *Za rulyom (Behind the Wheel),* the Soviet version of *Road and Track,* had part of its masthead in English, for no other reason than to pay homage to the country of Henry Ford.

At a remove of fifty years, and especially with the intervention of all those Cold-War thunderbolts hurled in the direction of capitalism, it's hard to appreciate Ford's reputation in Russia—not only the intensity but the scope. It went well beyond that of a mere automaker. He was given an approving entry in the 1936 edition of the *Bolshaya Entsiklopediya,* which was almost the secular equivalent of sanctification, and his name appeared alongside those of Marx and Lenin on banners carried aloft in workers' parades. The Russian version of Ford's autobiography became a best-seller after it was endorsed in *Pravda.*

Ford reached such heights because this quintessential capitalist could—with a little fiddling—be made to fit into the Soviet philosophy of labor. Ford insisted no less fervently than Lenin that physical work was ennobling. His argument that the average man using "honest logic" could solve all problems without the aid of experts was also welcome justification for a regime that had lately expelled or exterminated many intellectuals. Most congenial of all were Ford's ideas about the rationalization of the workplace, for example his assembly-line methods and time-and-motion studies. The Soviet Union, which was desperate to put its economy on a stable footing, found the allure of a well-run workplace irresistible. The Central Labor Institute put its authority behind the concept of "the scientific organization of labor," and *fordizm* and *fordizatsiya* became inspirational slogans.

*Fordizm* did not carry the day without opposition. Interpreted in one way, after all, it implied the oppression of the worker, precisely the capitalistic exploitation that communism was meant to transcend. It was a time when public debate was still allowed, and voices were raised in protest. "Detroit has the greatest number of divorces. The Ford system makes workers impotent," Vladimir Mayakovsky announced after touring the Ford plant in 1925. The detail is Mayakovsky being characteristically shocking, but the idea that *fordizm* was a real danger was widespread.

Lenin wavered, unable at first to accept the exploitation that *fordizm* implied. "The 'Scientific' system of squeezing out sweat," he called it in an article. But ultimately he put production requirements over ideological scruples, and most of those in ruling circles concurred. The director of the Central Labor Institute, Alexander Gastev, looked forward to a "Soviet Americanism . . . a new flowering America" in Russia.

The Bolsheviks required a new worker psychology as well as better management techniques, and for this too they turned to America as the best model. To study it close up, numerous Russians took jobs in American industry, then recorded their experiences in popular articles with titles like "At the Workbench at Ford" and "What I Saw in America." Running through these reports is a note of bewilderment, as the writers rummage through heaps of mundane detail in the hope of discovering the secret of America's success. ". . . when there is some unexpected interruption, a worker is not supposed to stand about idly," wrote one visiting engineer about the Ford plant at River Rouge. "He quickly arms himself with a rag, which is provided daily, and occupies himself with cleaning up his machine. I saw one worker who polished his machine so elegantly that it shone like a samovar." In addition to such light housekeeping, there was, of course, the exhausting routine of the assembly line. T. S. Bardin, who later became head of the technological division of the Academy of Sciences, worked in a Gary, Indiana, steel plant, putting in shifts ten to twelve hours long and coming home each night feeling, as he put it, "like a squeezed-out turnip." A squeezed-out turnip was the condition Soviet workers had also to aspire to, if the economy was ever to be turned around.

For a time after the Revolution, American workers and technicians were actively recruited by the Society for Technological Aid to Soviet Russia, the official Soviet agency in New York. The Americans were to have two roles: filling gaps in the native labor force and—as important—serving as a living model of a correct work ethic. Lenin expressed his faith in American methods by handing over management of the AMO auto parts factory in Moscow to a contingent of fifty Americans who had worked on the Ford assembly lines. The move caused controversy despite Lenin's authority—the AMO works was a prominent and critical facility, not to be given over lightly to foreign hands. But the American ideal eventually carried the day.

Those were the glory days of the Revolution, and the government believed that hundreds of thousands of American workers would come to the Soviet Union to help speed socialism forward. About fifteen thousand showed up, far below the projections but still a substantial number. A fair percentage were returning emigrants who had not found in America what they had hoped for, or their children who were drawn by ancestral ties. Ideological solidarity drew a fair number, especially members of the American Communist party. And still others simply hoped for a lucrative payday. Americans commanded high wages, and they took all they deserved and sometimes more—many inflated their credentials, knowing the Soviets were in no position to argue.

For all the traffic, however, the influence of American workers on the Soviet workplace was circumscribed. Chaotic conditions were partially responsible. One group from Oregon that intended to establish a fish-canning plant had several carloads of equipment and belongings misdirected immediately on arrival, not to be recovered for months; they had to face the Murmansk winter with a few hand tools and in their light summer clothing. Another group had plans to form a self-supporting tractor unit as a way of circumventing the nightmarish Soviet supply system; they were ordered to Perm, eighty miles from railroad transport and in an area where the poor land made farming almost impossible. When their long-awaited harvester-combine arrived from America, the local authorities installed it in a shop window for purposes of demonstration, leaving the Americans to reap their harvest with sickles. Such misadventures were duplicated many times over and added up to a mordant lesson—chaos is the natural Russian climate, no matter how the political winds are blowing.

Official policy also limited the influence of the American worker. Though the government had invited the Americans to come, it resisted giving them a free hand once they arrived. Project Kuzbas (the acronym formed from Kuznets Basin, in Siberia) was a striking instance of this ambivalence. Originally designated an "autonomous economic colony," it was administered entirely by Americans, who introduced the methods of American industry (including regular time shifts and cost accounting). Though there were indications of success, Moscow began to rein in the Americans almost immediately. A Russian director was installed. The promised autonomy was eliminated. Reflecting the regime's second thoughts,

Lenin pronounced William ("Big Bill") Haywood, one of the guiding spirits of the project, to be "half anarchistic." The term, with its implication of uncontrollable independence, was among the severest judgments of the time.

The Americans with Project Kuzbas were of a sort virtually guaranteed to irritate a bureaucracy aiming for uniformity. Most were from the ranks of the Industrial Workers of the World (Haywood was the union's former president), and their syndicalist background made them sensitive to bureaucratic meddling. But virtually all the American workers who came to Russia bristled at the regime's heavy-handedness. When Moscow moved to reorganize the labor force into hierarchical groupings, the wry response of one of the Kuzbas Americans—"Workers of the world unite—yeah, and then get divided into sixteen categories"—could have been uttered by any of the 15,000 Americans in the country. From the Soviet point of view, the Americans seemed increasingly a trouble not worth the effort. By the mid-1930s most American workers had been banished and the slogans extolling *fordizm* expunged. The regime still meant to create a disciplined labor force, more disciplined, indeed, than the original American model, but it would do so under a banner of its own devising. The legend of the selfless, hard-driving steelworker Alexey Stakhanov (purportedly emulated by thousands of Stakhanovite workers around the country) replaced the myth of Henry Ford. But though the names and faces changed, the ideal of American efficiency lived on.

In most of the world, America's reputation is not what it was. These days no one marvels at the efficiency of our assembly lines. No stories circulate about our workers' discipline and productivity, except ironic ones. Henry Ford is dead, and if his methods are still used, it is without jubilation. Some recent innovations could have been thought up precisely to set Ford's spirit to gnashing its teeth—motivating workers by providing health clubs, letting workers set the pace of jobs, introducing (or pretending to introduce) egalitarian relationships between bosses and workers, all the frills and embroidery that mark the workplace of late capitalism.

In the Soviet Union, ideas about work have also changed. The old exhortations to build a new society fall on deaf ears. Workers consider long hours for little wages a burden and not a necessary part of the grand communist project. I heard comments that would have been unthinkable just a few years ago. The shrill complaints were less shocking than small asides woven into everyday conversations; disenchantment is so much the norm that it needs no emphasis.

After deplaning at Sheremetyovo Airport outside Moscow, I had dragged my bags onto a crowded elevator; it was one of those contraptions with doors at front and back opening alternately at each floor, and the crowd grew exasperated at being pushed first one way and then another as each new passenger entered. "Forward, citizens, forward," demanded a heavyset woman who was trying to maneuver three large suitcases onto the elevator. "Forward, citizens, forward to a marvelous future," came the echo from the old man next to me. That measures the distance the Soviet Union has come: what was once the main inspirational slogan of communism, the promise that today's hard efforts would yield marvelous rewards in the near future, is now reduced to a weary joke. Russia is in crisis, and is eager to listen to new ideas meant to revitalize the workplace, including—once again—American ideas. Either they have not heard of our recent economic problems or, more likely, they are turning to us as someone intuitively edges toward a faint echo of an old favorite tune.

The joint venture, the favored form for bringing Russians and Americans together to do business, is a big step for a country that for much of history has gone it alone. In fact, so many joint ventures have been proposed that what only a few years ago was being hailed as breathtakingly innovative already seems old hat. I was told that Georgi Arbatov, who in his capacity as director of the Institute of United States and Canada monitors many joint venture proposals, now hardly shows interest when he meets with the principals to hear their plans. But he reportedly jumped up in excitement when he learned of the deal that CRT was proposing.

CRT is a successful arbitrage firm in Chicago. Its founder, Joe Ritchie, is a figure from the classic American dream. A former bus driver and a prison guard, he parlayed enthusiasm and a stomach for risk-taking into millions on the stock market. The 1980s emendation to the classic American dream is a penchant for pop psychology, manifested mainly in the suggestion that work is good healthy fun, no more than leisure-time pleasure by other means. Ritchie is a born-again Christian, and likes to believe that the principles of his faith have a place in his company. CRT defines its organization as an "egoless team sport built on personal character." Hierarchical authority, or at least its more visible signs, has been toned down. Everyone is on a first-name basis. There are no dress codes. The explicit model of behavior is the family (more exactly, perhaps, the well-behaved family); CRT executives like to note that several of the top officers are related through marriage—proof, presumably, that the company takes the idea of the family very seriously.

Arbatov's enthusiasm may have been sparked by the prospect of an American millionaire ready to pump money into the Russian economy, but it's a fair assumption that CRT's organizational style had an influence also. The Soviet Union is desperate for new ideas about the workplace. CRT's proposal was approved, and a joint venture—to develop software in Moscow and sell it in America—was established. To underscore the spirit of cooperation, it was called Dialog.

I visited Dialog's offices in a building off Manège Square, in what had been the main hall of Moscow University before that institution decamped for the Lenin Hills in the 1950s. The building was erected in the eighteenth century, when Russia undertook a crash course to bring itself to intellectual parity with the West. It's full of blind alleys, odd crannies, and false entries; it has an organic quality, as if more rooms and wings had agglutinated each time

Russia ventured into another new area of knowledge. The building appears desolate now, the windows dusty and the paint on the walls peeling, but there is still a palpable whiff of livelier times: in the tsarist era, this had often been an outpost of intellectual daring. It struck me as a good place for Dialog to explore the new world of American business techniques.

In a large room on the second floor some forty people were scurrying around, jotting down notes, talking animatedly. There were computer terminals on most of the randomly situated desks, and folding chairs were scattered around the room. The people seemed as little fixed in any one place as the furniture. They formed themselves into small groups, argued for a few minutes, then broke up and re-formed in new deployments, with everyone dragging his chair along behind him. It was a picture of either perfect collegiality or pure chaos. It did not resemble any Soviet workplace I had ever seen.

The director of Dialog is Peter Zverlov, formerly assistant to the head of the Kamskiy Automobile Factory before he sensed which way the economic winds were blowing. The old ways had to be overhauled if Russia was to survive, he told me. Trying to find a place where we could talk with a degree of peace, Zverlov picked up one of the folding chairs, motioned for me to do likewise, and led me to a corner where we established a makeshift office. We even brought a makeshift anteroom with us. A man and woman who had been waiting to speak to Zverlov took their chairs, followed along behind us, and sat down at the same polite distance as before.

Zverlov had a gracious manner. He was gracious by any standard, but especially by those of his calling. Russian managers are notoriously rude, sporting surliness as if it were a badge of honor. They treat every encounter as an opportunity to insinuate their rank. But Zverlov made himself approachable. Our conversation was continuously interrupted by requests that he sign papers or answer questions. At one point, he rushed across the room to hug a birthday celebrant. He waited his turn courteously, and no one thought of ceding him priority. His every word and act seemed democratized, spun into a fine web of equality. Only the couple waiting to talk to Zverlov, who I now noticed were middle-aged and sedately dressed, seemed excluded from the prevailing style. They sat silently, shoulders slumped, and looking as if they were prepared to sit hours more in the same pose. Perhaps Zverlov overlooked them because they appeared so out of place in the Dialog office.

Zverlov told me how Dialog had got started. "I met Joe Ritchie at an international conference. We talked, he liked our ideas. He said, 'Here, take five million—if it doesn't work out I'll have made a mistake.' "

"The legend of the generous American millionaire come true," I remarked.

"Oh yes, but it's not all one-way. We bring something that I think America can use—our brains. The ability to think abstractly. We have a tradition of pure science, of pure math. It's no accident we have so many chess champions, you know," he said, staking out Russia's territory in this partnership. "What we lack is organizational skill."

I remarked that there seemed to be an unusual amount of communication among the people in the room, sudden conferences, information shouted from one corner to the other. Zverlov replied, "A lot comes from the CRT philosophy. But we are learning. It takes a while to shift gears after generations of authoritarianism."

Zverlov continued to expound Dialog's philosophy; he probably had said the same words many times before, but his excitement still seemed genuine. "We think of ourselves as a group enterprise. Someone who is egotistical could upset the balance and so we have to be very careful who we hire. We've studied CRT interview techniques very carefully. Our interviewers are trained to look for clues. For example, if someone becomes annoyed when the interview is interrupted, we know he is an egotist. You develop an instinct. An ordinary conversation can be very revealing if you know what to look for. We need people who are willing to give up the old ways of doing things."

Zverlov saw me graciously to the door, and as I said good-bye I took one last look around Dialog. It was such a far cry from the old ways that even the musty, papery odor typical of Russian offices was absent. Perhaps here, I told myself, was the Russian workplace of the future. But I should probably have kept my enthusiasm in check.

A few days later the friend who had introduced me to Zverlov invited me to his home to meet a young woman who had recently applied for a job at Dialog. She was bright and obviously intelligent, so it was a surprise to hear she had been turned down. I asked why.

"The interviewer didn't like me, that's all."

"But why not?"

"He just didn't. Perhaps he didn't like the way I walked." As a joke, she got up and promenaded around the living room. "Looks normal, doesn't it?" she called out. "But perhaps he saw something we cannot."

As I listened to her rueful tale, the picture of Dialog that I had in my mind shifted slightly, but crucially. Zverlov was still the gracious director, the office still bustled with energy, but the fact that employees were chosen according to the arbitrary tenets of pop psychology cast a shadow.

Pop psychology is bad enough in America, but we have over the years learned to live with it. Our workplaces, like our society, have developed a sag and looseness that accommodates outlandish practices. But Russia has a long way to go before it can master our little tricks of flexibility. I remembered that middle-aged couple waiting for an audience with Zverlov. They were, I realized, just like that stock figure of Russian literature, the petitioner, who cooled his heels in anterooms of both the tsarist and Soviet bureaucracies until authority beckoned. Dialog presents itself as progressive, and in many ways it is, but Russia's old traditions—the whims of authority and the acquiescence of subordinates—have a power that cannot be easily brushed aside.

A case can be made, barely, that Russia acted reasonably in the 1920s and 1930s when it tried to borrow American ideas about the workplace—had not America covered much (though not all!) of the economic ground that Russia would pass through on the way to communism? The convergence was slight and finally proved illusory, but at the time it seemed an arguable possibility. Since then, however, our economic paths have moved much farther apart. If the economic relationship between America and Russia was once like a melodrama, full of false hopes, missed connections, and un-expected exits, it is now in danger of turning into something like a farce with mismatched partners and silly pratfalls. Russia has many stages of economic and social development to pass through before it can absorb things like CRT trendy ideas about the workplace. Wishful thinking will not nullify the law of unequal development.

In 1705, as part of his effort to alter traditional mores, Peter the Great permitted the importation of Virginia tobacco. Before that, smoking had been, at least technically, a capital offense, and was engaged in secretly if at all; now Russians could puff away on their oxhorns in public. American goods had arrived on a cloud of per-missiveness and modernity, two qualities with which they would continue to be associated.

Today's Russians are astonishingly familiar with the things out of which we construct our daily life. I had mixed feelings—part national pride that they showed interest, part amazement that they bothered—when I realized a few knew more about American prod-ucts than I did. Though television and movies help to spread the word, many Russians acquire their expertise simply by being ded-icated tourist watchers. Over the years they became very good at a sort of sartorial exegesis, knowingly comparing styles of raincoats or reckoning the value of a belt, and now they have also learned to assess the knickknacks of our high-tech world, from digital watches to Walkmans. The space in front of a tourist hotel resem-bles a reviewing stand, as Russians lounge around on the hoods of parked cars at all hours of the day and night waiting for America's *dernier cri* to appear, even if it's only the version displayed by retired schoolteachers on tour. Dressing nondescriptly or carrying less than the required tonnage of electronic paraphernalia, you can easily feel that you have let down the American way of life.

American goods have a long-standing reputation for utility, going back to the prerevolutionary period when the Russian infantryman trudged into battle shouldering his trusty "Berdanka," the affectionate nickname given the rifle designed by General Hiram Berdan of Connecticut. Today, Russia may be one of the last places in the world where "made in America" represents an endorsement. But it's not only utility that is important. American goods have an aura, a quasi-mystical connotation. Walking from my hotel along Gorky Street to Pushkin Square, a distance of half a mile, I had offers for my Reebok shoes, my Lands' End briefcase, my Timex watch, all those items that turned me into a walking billboard. No one bid for my coat, sturdy and warm but lacking some mark of its American provenance. Russians want the aura.

And they'll take it in almost any form. Dom Mody (House of Fashion) on Marx Prospect has a luxurious air, not less imposing than the Fifth Avenue boutiques it closely resembles. There was the same hush, the same solicitous but slightly haughty salespeople. Soviet fashion used to be a hilarious oxymoron, but apparently no longer. To my untutored eye, the mannequins' dresses were as fancy as those in the West, the only difference being that here the price tag was broken down into the cost of the labor and of the material—in the Soviet Union, Marx's Law of Surplus Value must be acknowledged even in the realm of high fashion. Dom Mody is the home base of Serge Zaitsev, the Soviet Union's most adventuresome designer. He has had several shows abroad and, so it is reported, a contract with a California distributor. I strolled out of the main showroom into an adjoining display hall where there was a bulletin board with news clippings affixed. These were reviews of Zaitsev's shows in America, from *The New York Times* and *Women's Wear Daily*. Remarkably, the critical opinions were unfavorable in the extreme. Apparently what counts is not what

America says about Russia's consumer goods, but that it says anything. Suffer the scorn; perhaps some of America's magic will rub off in the process.

Dom Mody is an exceptional phenomenon, a Russian clothing store that offers stylish clothes (though at prices few Russians can afford). In most stores the racks are empty or filled with items so ill-fitting and poorly made they are a joke. This has often been the way it is, and people used just to shrug in weary acceptance. Lately a new psychology seems to have taken hold. One of the most popular events in town was the *Pikant-shou,* a spectacle consisting of a parade of deadpan performers wearing the sorts of clothes available in the state stores. When the dancers attired themselves in dowdy pajamas, corsets, and underwear and moved into a formal tango, it brought down the house. "How shameful that they should put on a spectacle in such costume," said an elderly lady during intermission. "How shameful that we should all have to wear such costumes every day of our lives," came the reply from a passing teenager. That measures the quality of despair. Russians now feel keenly what they lack; they can define their complaints precisely and even enact them on the stage, which would have been unthinkable a few years ago. It's become a society where the appetite for quality goods has been refined to an exquisite degree, but where getting one's hands on them is still largely impossible—a consumer society without consumer goods. No wonder America is viewed through the distorting prism of deep longing.

It's tricky trying to summon up the symbolic meanings of physical objects. Concentrate your stare at a VCR and it will likely remain just a VCR. The context is all. Stare at an American VCR in the home of some lucky Russian and it may begin to hum with implications. Politics, which colors so much of American-Soviet relations, has little to do with this. Even loyal Party members have over the years fallen under the spell of American goods. "He was a Bolshevik," declared Theodore Dreiser upon meeting the film director Sergei Eisenstein. "His room, one of a flat of six rooms, occupied Moscow-style by six families, was very small for New York or for a leading moving picture director but spacious for Moscow. To make it more habitable or presentable, he himself had decorated the walls with a series of fantastic bull's-eye convolutions of color, and above his desk, for purposes of ornamentation, I suppose, was an American placard advertising a new cream separator." What did Eisenstein see when he looked at the separator? Did he consider it pure ornamentation, as Dreiser thought? Or did it remind him of his film *The General Line* with its famous sequence depicting the first use of a separator on a Soviet collective farm? Or did he see in it, as I believe, some messy amalgam of meanings, adumbrations of an alternative world, a not-hereness that made his life in Russia stand out more sharply? Eisenstein lived a full life in Soviet society—but he may have needed to gauge its daily meanings by using this American standard. Many loyal Russian citizens appear to need some such measuring device.

Though a fascination with American products need not imply a repudiation of the Soviet system, the government has always assumed the worst. Over the years it has tried various strategies to dim their allure. In the early days of Bolshevism, when ideological fervor was at a peak, the Party line was that in America consumer products served to keep the working masses from thinking about the class struggle. Maksim Gorky, soon to become the first head of the Soviet Writers Union, had set the tone in 1905 when he announced that Americans had been reduced to "blind tools" serving the "yellow devil" of money. Capitalism had continually to foster consumerism in order to disguise the moral vacuum at its heart. "Never before," Gorky averred, "have a people seemed so insignificant, so enslaved." This sort of apocalyptic language was music to the ears of Soviet propagandists, and they set their apparatus to grinding out endless variations on the motif. The propaganda persuaded many; it is also true that over the years its extremism aroused suspicion. It was hard to imagine an America all that bad. Sometimes the propaganda only made American goods more desirable, items whose allure grew more intense to the degree that they were officially scorned. In 1929, the Moscow Art Theater staged Ilya Ehrenburg's *The D.E. Trust*. The plot—how a scheme by American capitalists to control Europe is thwarted by the proletariat—seemed ideal propaganda, but in performance something went wrong. Scenes of communists building a new world caused yawns, while those of dandified bankers dancing foxtrots to a jazz band brought down the house. A new fad took hold: an enterprising tobacco company began to produce D.E. cigarettes, which proved very popular with the young and adventurous. Then and later, the Soviet government found that trying to block the aura of America from reaching the population was as difficult as trying to block smoke. By the 1960s and 1970s, it is said, readers of *Pravda* were ignoring the gloating captions under photos of American unemployment lines and instead were scrutinizing with envy the clothes worn by even the most unfortunate in the capitalist economy.

With the rise of Gorbachev, the perspective on America has undergone a sea change. The old slogans have been discarded. "The class struggle?" the editor of *Moskovskie novosti* observed. "That's in the past, words that have no meaning today. That was for another time." We sat in his office overlooking Pushkin Square. A secretary deferentially brought in some tea and—an unexpected amenity— cookies. "What is wrong with consumerism anyway?" he asked. "Consumerism can mean that I can have a nice study at home with a good typewriter, which only makes me work better." His every statement seemed designed to top the previous one, a demonstration of the ideological reflex in its death throes. "Comfort need not be in contradiction to proper social activity—comfort can make these activities more productive," he said, seeming to sink a bit deeper into his leather armchair. He told me of his recent trip to America. "I liked it, except for one thing. My hosts at *The Trenton Times*, perhaps to show me that not everything in America is comfortable, put me into an apartment without air-conditioning. And it was a hot summer, I can tell you." He was just kidding, he assured me; still, it was astonishing to hear an editor of a Soviet newspaper criticize America for not being bourgeois enough.

*Moskovskie novosti* is particularly iconoclastic, but ideological fervor against American consumerism has waned in all Soviet media, sometimes to the vanishing point. *Krokodil,* a journal with a slashing, aggressive reputation, now has far more cartoons mocking domestic shortages than American decadence. (A typical one: A Soviet everyman dressed up as Prometheus in full flight is observed by Zeus, who says, "Let him go, with those matches he'll never start a fire.") Comedians on state-run television joke about the shoddiness of Russian goods. Even *Izvestia,* a bastion of conservatism, occasionally complains and murmurs about American successes.

On the few occasions when the media reverts to its old combativeness, its weapons are a far cry from the fire-and-brimstone style developed by Gorky. On the television in my hotel room I saw a sketch that satirized American consumerism. To the sound of Whitney Houston singing "I Want to Dance with Somebody," a group of young people rush from store to store, trying on expensive shoes and jewelry. The music and the zippy editing give the sketch the feel of a slightly underproduced American advertisement, though it's not clear what is being sold. Only at the end does any point of view emerge. A voice declares, "That's how it is done: tomorrow you will want to buy things you didn't want yesterday, and the day after you will absolutely need these things." The tone is wry, almost apologetic; there is a sense that other conclusions could as easily be drawn from the sketch. This is propaganda as theater of weariness, and it may after all be the most effective approach for the times.

When I heard that three members of the Industrial Designers Society of America passing through Moscow were going to give a lecture and slide show, I decided to attend. The occasion suggested a particularly intense confrontation of Russian and American styles. On a dreary, wet afternoon I made my way to the Soviet Society of Designers on Kiselny Lane.

Consumer America was on parade from the moment the society's director completed his introduction. The speakers approaching the lectern, it was stunningly clear, were people who not only would discuss contemporary American style but would also embody it. What they wore—double-breasted blazers, boldly striped shirts, shoes of a Continental style, ties with a rainbow of color—would perhaps have gone unnoticed on Madison Avenue but was completely out of step on Kiselny Lane; doublets and codpieces would not have raised more eyebrows. The audience, consisting of some two dozen of the leading Soviet designers, wore the adult citizen's standard uniform of a dark, shapeless suit and white shirt. Most had a morose expression to match, as if they anticipated having to sit through something unpleasant.

After the speakers had made some offhand prefatory remarks in a colloquial style that largely defeated the translator's efforts, the lights were turned off and a sequence of slides flashed on the screen. They showed the recent achievements of American industrial design: sleek office furniture, dripless teakettles, futuristic sunglasses, all in gaudy technicolor. It was a heady mix. It made me wonder about the motives—was this perhaps some sort of *pour épater le prolétariat* impulse? The audience, however, showed little emotion. Most stared fixedly ahead with a show of bland attention. The best America had to offer, they seemed to say, left them unmoved.

Finally a slide showing an object of surpassing unusualness, a sleek bicycle with spokeless wheels, moved an efficient-looking woman in the first row to speak. "Who would buy such a thing?" she asked.

"It's an attempt to make an everyday object into sculpture," the American speaker replied. Not waiting to see how this information was received, he moved on to slides of a space-age salad bowl, a sleek car interior, and a television mounted on a movable robot that was capable of following its master through all the rooms of a house.

"I should state," he said in a confidential tone, "that these are not plans but reality. All the items shown here today are actually in production, not just on the drawing board."

"Ah well," the courtly director of the society piped up from his seat in the front row, "I should state that all the items we will show you are emphatically not in production." The sardonic remark roused some in the audience to weak laughter, and a few whispered to each other. But the swell of activity subsided quickly, as if it had taken all the audience's energy.

The American, riding out the interruption with a thin smile, returned to his prepared notes. The next slides were of an airline terminal full of white plastic and wraparound windows and neon lights. "A moving sidewalk gets you from gate to gate," he said. "Careful attention to detail can make even an airline terminal an attractive place and traveling a fun experience."

The translator hesitated, then uncertainly ventured a phrase. "Careful design can have a strong emotional effect," he said.

A few in the audience who knew English hooted at his inadequate translation, but good-naturedly. It was clear that they sympathized with the difficulty of trying to put the concept of "a fun experience" into Russian. "We are not used to such a rich diet," was the comment of the fellow beside me. "If you eat kasha every day it becomes hard to describe the taste of caviar."

The American at the lectern seemed not to notice the commotion in the audience and proceeded to the next slides. They showed the perfume department at Neiman Marcus and were stunning. The place looked more like a sumptuous boudoir than a store. Even in the resplendent context of what had been previously shown, these slides stood out. The audience was silent, but it was clear their attitude of indifference had been shattered. I thought I heard a slight gasp off to my right.

Abruptly, a strong, challenging voice broke the tension. "And where are the people, the customers and sales clerks?" It was the efficient-looking woman again, this time speaking with the happy assurance of a detective who has broken an airtight alibi at last. "Is business always so bad?"

"This was shot early in the morning, before the store was open," came the answer. "That way the photographer could be certain there would be no interference."

Many in the audience nodded, but knowingly and even with an occasional wink. The woman who asked the question turned to say a few words to the director, after which they both laughed. There was a lot of fairly loud whispering. Reticence was replaced by a new assertiveness, as in a classroom where awe of the teacher gives way to pranks. The Neiman Marcus store, which at first had stunned the Russians, turned out to be a tool to explain away America's grandeur. Russia has a long tradition (going back to the notorious Potemkin Villages of Catherine the Great's time) of the impressive facade, the luxurious oasis in the midst of desolation, the fancy bauble that is not for public sale—the audience knew very well that such things do not constitute a real country. As the lecture moved toward a conclusion, it seemed that a working equilibrium had been established. The Americans flaunted their extravagances. The Russians watched with a knowing curiosity; they applauded occasionally, politely.

It would have ended like that, I suppose, a polite stalemate that left any deeper feelings undisturbed, except that at the end of his presentation the lecturer took an unexpected tack. His tone modulating from formality to bluff camaraderie, he announced that he wanted to close on a personal note. Instead of slides showing objects produced by industrial designers, he would show some snapshots of his own life. His Boston office, his happy family with dog, even his shiny car near a suburban garage now appeared on the screen. It was a picture of an upper-middle-class American life, very comfortable, even plush, but with enough rough edges to appear incontrovertibly real.

The audience fell silent, a deep, palpably sad silence this time, and I sensed some ultimate deflation of spirit. Though the American had probably been doing no more than trying to find a friendly coda, the effect was devastating. The common appurtenances of his work and his domestic life might not have been as luxurious as a life filled with dripless kettles and TV robots, but they were splendid enough, and more enviable, too, since they seemed aspects of the average American's lot. The slides implied a nation that was from end to end prosperous, a seamless web of comfort.

We moved on to slides of the American's summer house in Rhode Island, shot from different angles to show the wraparound porch, the widow's walk on the roof, the marvelous ocean vista. For a final picturesque effect, there was a slide of a ramshackle wooden fence following the curve of the dunes.

"Now that fence," said a young man in the back row quite loudly, "that fence is something we have in the Soviet Union also."

The audience erupted into loud laughter, a rolling wave of sound that seemed to come from the pit of their stomachs. Under cover of this merry self-irony, the Russians made their escape from the room.

America's most common products—items we use unthinkingly as we follow our daily rounds—can acquire a surprising moral heft when transported to Russia. Once in Leningrad I opened my red-and-yellow umbrella against a sudden shower, causing an old baba to stop in midstride and shout in my direction, *"Kuda ty, na festival* (Where are you off to, a festival)?"* The incident gave me the thrill of astonishing the natives, but also made me feel embarrassed at the cheapness of my pleasure—cheap morally and materially as well, since I had bought the umbrella for three dollars from a peddler on Broadway. At other times I felt reduced to no more than a providing agent. Chance encounters, even those that began promisingly, often turned out to be only preambles to requests for Marlboros. Even friendships were distorted. If friends lacked something, why not provide it? But the items—cigarettes, tonic water, records, jeans—seemed to occupy some uncertain ground between gifts and supplies, leaving everyone feeling awkward.

On departing Russia, I made a present of the red-and-yellow umbrella to a lady friend who had admired it. She was someone, in fact, who had as if by magic managed to assemble from the meager Soviet market a sophisticated style, and besides, she had never asked me for the umbrella directly. But a year in the Soviet Union had made me sensitive to every hint of material desire. I gave the umbrella to a mutual acquaintance to pass along to my friend, being too ashamed to give her such a paltry thing personally, yet not wanting to take the chance that I had missed any wistful murmurs.

One cloudy Saturday, I took a ride out to the Riga Market. The market is in one of Moscow's outlying neighborhoods; the territory it occupies in the national economy is less easily defined—unofficial but tolerated. Within a conglomeration of peddler stands and prefab huts, goods that are not available anywhere else can be had at black-market prices. The mood is of a frontier town on the make. The hawkers grab at passersby and maneuver them to the merchandise. There are offers to squeeze the watermelon, stroke the leather belts, try on the jeans. The bargaining produces a persistent sound, a low-pitched, frenetic hum. You don't so much walk in the Riga Market as get carried along by the surge of crowds pressing forward in search of the best deal.

It was a textbook example of the hunger for things, but there was also a distinctly American air to it. If there is a plague of consumerism loose in the land, the Riga Market argued that the virus is American. The jeans and denim jackets sported the names of second-line Stateside manufacturers and the dyed T-shirts were decorated with Michael Jackson's image. One peddler had cleared a space and was hawking wallets containing photos of Sylvester Stallone, Arnold Schwarzenegger, and, improbably, the 1950s movie star Janet Leigh; the selling point was that the wallet had a device "invented in America just recently" to secure the bills in place and keep them "always clean, always neat."

"Those Shtatniki [Stateniks]," said a woman beside me, her eyes widening with awe, "what will they think of next?"

Inside the large central building, where the smell of garlic and cabbage was like an assault, a swarthy, bearded peddler in a leather bomber jacket pulled me over to his vegetable stand. "German?"

he asked. "Italian?" When I said I was American, his face lit up as if he had struck gold. Holding me by the arm in a firm grip, he proceeded to recite the names of all the basketball stars he could recall. Michael Jordan, Kareem Abdul-Jabbar, Magic Johnson—he made the names sound like a poem about some fabled land. "Now," he announced, "you will give me a souvenir. Perhaps a watch?" He seemed to think he had earned it. He settled for a ballpoint pen.

I left the Riga Market feeling something was seriously askew. The rage for American goods struck me as grotesque, even unethical, but I would have had a hard time trying to explain my reaction—don't Russians, after all, no less than other peoples, deserve the things they believe will make life comfortable or pleasurable or just plain amusing? It was not until later that week, as I was waiting for a friend outside the Taganka Theater, that my misgivings crystallized. I still could not have put them into a neat sentence, but I now had an image I could point to instead.

I was passing the time by looking at the crowds exiting the nearby metro, and my eye caught one elderly woman with a kerchief tied around her head. In her manner and appearance she was Russian through and through, probably not many years removed from scrabbling out a farm existence; but, incongruously, she carried a plastic shopping bag with a picture of a man in a fancy sweater fishing in a cool mountain stream, his evident contentment derived in unclear proportion from the rod he was wielding and the Salem cigarette he was smoking. What skein of events had put into her hand this image of bourgeois paradise, so distant from her own life? From American tourist to hotel maid to shopgirl to this elderly woman, the shopping bag must have followed some circuitous route, probably never eliciting much comment but never discarded either. It somehow floated aimlessly on the currents of Soviet life, an item simultaneously valuable and meaningless.

## three

# Tracking
# the
# American
# Soul

It is an aspect of what might be called the commissar mentality, and it takes the form of a dogged refusal to forgive Americans their nationality. Bureaucrats and ideologues exhibit the tendency, but so do hotel clerks, Intourist guides, shopgirls, in fact all sorts of Russians. Customs guards, who anyway have antagonism bred into them, like fighting cocks, are especially provoked by Americans. I've had my share of run-ins with them. My luggage has been turned inside out, my books scrutinized, a painting by a Soviet friend confiscated. I've been questioned sharply and patted down briskly. I've been told to remove my jacket, my shoes. In a small room in Sheremetyovo Airport, a customs official considered for a few minutes before finally deciding to allow me to keep my pants on.

Once on the Leningrad–Helsinki train, my wife and I were searched and interrogated for forty-five minutes. The other occupants of our compartment were ordered into the corridor; presumably more space was needed to throw our belongings about, but it might as well have been because some heinous rite was about to be performed, not fit for the eyes of men. They went painstakingly through our suitcases, tapping them for false bottoms. They looked through our papers, transcribing at random. Stupidly, I announced that if this went on much longer I would want to contact the United States consul.

"Your consul is hundreds of miles away, and you, you are here," the official in charge replied, his eyes narrowing to a feral focus, flat and with no hint of a thinking mind beyond. I felt a twinge in my stomach. It wasn't the prospect of any actual danger—Americans in Russia are rarely detained, even in periods of sharp political antagonism, and anyway I had broken no rules. But I did suddenly feel very far from home.

Afterward, once the train had crossed the border, some of the other passengers came over and thanked us for taking up so much time that the customs officials had none to spare for anyone else. A ten-member Finnish choir, returning from a tour of Novosibirsk, was especially grateful; Finns want as little as possible to do with their hated neighbors. By way of thanks, and also to celebrate departing Soviet territory, they took us into their compartment and serenaded us. Crammed amid ten robust Finns on the two bunks, with the songs bouncing off the metal walls, we felt the pleasure of finding an intimate link with passing strangers. The choir de-trained just outside of Helsinki, and, in a gesture worthy of an old musical operetta, deployed itself on the platform, singing lustily and waving when my wife and I leaned out the window. The jolly scene almost made up for the confrontation with the customs official—but not quite. It's not that easy to get over the anxiety of being in the power of someone who hates you with utter abstraction, not for any personal reasons but simply because of the accident of nationality.

The tendency to think of "American" as a category is widespread in Russia, even among those not unfavorably disposed. Russians seem determined to figure out our national character. Though most Russians rarely see an American, and never talk to one, they have managed to devise a balance sheet of our flaws and virtues. They tote up the traits and assume they've found the exemplary American. It's an odd perspective, and like creatures in fairy tales we may appear distanced and vivid at the same time. An actual encounter with an American is often only an opportunity to confirm the version Russians already carry in their heads. After meeting Mark Twain (in Paris in 1879), Ivan Turgenev wrote, "At last I have seen a real American, the first American who conforms to my idea of what an American should be. He was a true son (*krovny syn*) of his country." Some set of features, some image of what an American was, had taken hold in the national imagination. The definition of an American has changed over the years, but the belief that there is a specific American type has not. A century after Turgenev's comment, the Nobel Laureate Joseph Brodsky remarked of Robert Frost, "When I first read him, I thought it was a trick—he seemed such a perfect American poet someone must have made him up." Like Frost, all Americans are constantly measured against an ideal Russians have devised; unlike Frost, we often don't get passing grades.

On the third day of my stay I picked up the weekly *Nedelya* and noticed an article about Intourist, the official Soviet tourist agency. The title was *"Ob ulybke, po nauchnomu"* ("About Smiles, Scientifically"), and it was about ways of dealing with American tourists. A matter of special importance was that of smiling, when to and when not to. Americans like to be smiled at; they take offense at the Soviet citizen's unsmiling face, unaware that this is the normal workaday expression. The correspondent stated, "I have many times crisscrossed the United States, and I can testify that for Americans a smile between strangers is not only a gesture of politeness; its absence demonstrates ill-will." A smile, it seems, is part of the American national character, a sign of our ingenuousness and daffy optimism.

In the hotel dining room, I began to scrutinize my compatriots, watching their faces. Trying to get the stern maître d's attention, imploring a distracted waiter for more coffee, nodding and bowing themselves out of the room, the Americans did seem to smile a lot. But was it really a national characteristic or only the reasonable reactions of people far from home who must confront the sleepy

and vaguely threatening dragon that is the staff of a Russian restaurant? I resolved that I, at least, would not smile. I demanded, I
complained; I did not smile. But I doubt if my point was taken as
intended. The Russians probably decided that I was simply the
American Who Had Resolved Not to Smile.

Finding the key to the American character is a long-standing
mission. Even in the eighteenth century, when contact between the
two nations was slight and passing, Russians were determined to
stretch the meager evidence into the shape of a comprehensive
definition. In such circumstances, the few Americans who visited
Russia often made lasting impressions. Among these, John Ledyard
stands out. He was the first American to travel extensively through
the empire, and the first to penetrate Siberia. Ledyard had become
interested in Russia when he was a member of Captain Cook's
1776–80 expedition that crossed briefly into Siberia. In 1786, with
the moral and financial support of Thomas Jefferson, he set out on
an extravagant expedition of his own, intending to traverse Russia,
cross the Bering Strait to Alaska, and then to walk across North
America. To sustain him on the trek, he planned to take "two great
dogs, an Indian pipe and a hatchet."

On the very first leg of the journey, while still in Paris, Ledyard
ran into difficulty. Catherine the Great dismissed his itinerary as
"chimerical," and her government withheld providing a passport.
Exasperated, Ledyard set off without waiting for official sanction.
Upon reaching Sweden, he found that the Gulf of Bothnia had not
frozen over that year, thwarting his plan to sled across to Finland.
Typically, he hardly hesitated before taking an alternative route,
walking some 1,200 miles through isolated territory in the dead of
winter. It took him eight weeks. He arrived in St. Petersburg pen-
niless, disheveled, and without proper documents. The welcome
was not warm, but Ledyard's spirits did not flag. Jefferson, writing
to a mutual friend, noted, "I had a letter from Ledyard lately, dated
at St. Petersburg. He had but two shirts, and yet more shirts than
shillings. Still, he is determined to obtain the palm of being the

first circumambulator of the earth. He says that having no money, they kick him from place to place, and thus he expects to be kicked around the globe."

After two months of effort, Ledyard was somehow able to secure the passport required for internal travel in Russia and at once set off eastward. Traveling by horse-drawn coach, he reached Moscow in five days, paused briefly, then continued on through the central Urals, finally making Yakutsk, near Lake Baikal. In his diary he noted that he was "naked for want of cloaths [sic] & with only a guinea in my purse." Disregarding advice not to travel during the winter, Ledyard made his way to Irkutsk.

Here his journey came to an abrupt end. On the personal order of the empress, he was arrested and escorted back to Moscow, where he spent six weeks in detention. Various reasons have been advanced for the arrest. Rumors had circulated that Ledyard was a French spy; he seems to have been disorderly in both Irkutsk and Yakutsk, even challenging the local commandant to a duel; and, finally, he may have annoyed Catherine by going off on the expedition without her express consent. Whatever the cause, the arrest focused popular attention on his exploits.

Ledyard's journey fit neatly into the picture of the American that was growing in the Russian imagination, based on rumor, fantasy, and gossip. As this was eventually worked out, the American was restless, impatient with convention, willing to rise to any challenge. There was something reckless, even disreputable, about him; he emanated a whiff of notoriety. A prominent figure in 1820s St. Petersburg society, he was nicknamed "the American," thanks mainly to his having endured a crazy trek through the Aleutians— but his reputation as a gambler, rake, and cruel duelist made the epithet even more appropriate. To some Russians, America seemed wholly composed of individuals with qualities similar to these; when an acquaintance set sail for New York, Alexander Herzen wryly noted that he would no doubt disappear into an "ocean of swindlers, fortune hunters, and adventurers," perhaps even himself become "a cardsharp or a slave-holder."

The most renowned American trait, however, was a talent for the practical, a can-do urge, even if, as with Ledyard, this concluded in a can't-be-done shrug of the shoulders. American pragmatism had enjoyed a high reputation in Russia since Benjamin Franklin, and the settlement of the western wilderness, which Russians tended to see as a feat of engineering as well as of socialization, confirmed it. Fascination with American practicality was sparked by its perceived absence at home, a lack that everyone admitted caused problems but was nevertheless not always regretted. Russians were proud of their capacity for the grand gesture, and adhered to the corollary belief that too much attention to detail proved a smallness of soul. Using this standard, Americans were sometimes admired, but not often envied; to be like an American would have meant relinquishing an appreciation of life's sweep, a taste for the grandiloquent. The difference in sensibilities is summed up in an episode involving Major Robert Whistler (father of the painter) who was one of the American engineers invited to oversee construction of the Moscow–St. Petersburg railway line in the 1830s. Whistler inquired of Nicholas I where he wanted the tracks laid; whereupon the Tsar of All the Russias grabbed a straightedge, drew a line on the map between the two cities, and left the room satisfied he had answered the question fully.

Enter, circa 1850, the Cowboy. Here was a figure who brought into focus the conglomeration of traits associated with Americans. Generations of aristocrats and radicals alike were brought up on the novels of Mayne Reid and Zane Grey. Reading *The White Chief* or *Riders of the Purple Sage,* they fell under the spell of the American West. Vladimir Nabokov insisted that throughout his life he remembered the frontispiece of a Reid novel, which depicted a trussed-up criminal buried up to his chin in the torrid sand of the desert, presumably suffering this horrible fate for having challenged the cowboy hero.

The Russian perspective was kaleidoscopic. Viewed from one angle, the cowboy's behavior appeared alien. Russians preferred traditional, rule-bound duels to six-gun shoot-'em-ups, and they did not think it wise practice to bury trespassers up to their necks in sand. Moreover, for all his wildness, the cowboy was really a pragmatist, no more than a gussied-up social engineer trying to bring harmony to the local community. Russians tended to grander dreams. But when viewed from another angle, the cowboy could appear very familiar. He could even seem very like a Russian, or at least what a Russian might be if circumstances were slightly altered. Russia, in fact, had a popular fiction genre of its own that closely resembled the cowboy tale, with Siberia standing in for Texas and the Urals for the Dakota Badlands.

The American and Russian versions of the cowboy story have a common thread. In both, the hero is forced to find justice outside the established rule of law. "Nothing remained for me to do but fight in my own way," Deadwood Dick announces after an evil guardian seizes his inheritance and tries to kill him. In *Stenka Razin, an Ataman of the Bandits in the Reign of Aleksei Mikhailovich,* the hero takes to banditry after killing the son of a cossack chief who seduces his sister, and in *The Conquest of Siberian Kingdom,* the cossack leader Ermak is similarly a good man forced outside the law by circumstance. A distrust of established laws, a sensitivity to insult, a quickness to take revenge—these are the features that the two nations seemed to share.

The Russian and American versions of the outlaw-cowboy story usually end similarly, with the hero returning to the society whose mores he transgressed. But there is a difference in the treatment. The American hero does not usually seek pardon from official authority. He needs only the acceptance of his fellow citizens. Instead of turning himself in to the sheriff, Deadwood Dick walks into the town saloon and announces, "I have come to Eureka to lead an honest existence, and be a citizen among you." But the Russian hero looks to the state for forgiveness. Though he may not regret his life outside the law, he submits to the power of the tsar. Such obedience is not servility, but a matter of timing—accept the world as it is until it can be changed from top to bottom; live by the rules today in order to make a grand revolution tomorrow.

From the Russian perspective, it is the American hero who is cautious, satisfied to create an enclave of personal happiness for himself and a few fellow creatures. He is not an adventurer of the spirit but a pragmatist with an altruistic bent.

These may seem like fine distinctions, but the Russian view of Americans is shot through with fine distinctions. They grant the similarities between themselves and us even as they insist on ultimate differences. Russians are direct, while Americans—Russians insist—are naive. Russians are impatient with empty formalities, but they profess shock at how little Americans understand basic rules of etiquette. (They take as all too typical John Randolph's remarks at his first appearance at the imperial court in 1824 in his capacity as ambassador: "How are you, Emperor?" he remarked, with a familiarity that shocked those present, "How is Madame?") Russians and Americans equally seize life's pleasures, but Russians believe their excesses have a philosophical point, whereas we merely indulge ourselves—American characters in Soviet films seem never to be without a glass of scotch in their hands, drinking continually but never exploding in the extravagant manner that is the hallmark of Russian narratives.

Americans are a standard Russians often measure themselves against, usually to their advantage. This posture, however, has often proved awkward. A noble character deserves a well-ordered society to live in, and Russian society has long been embarrassingly backward. Worse still, Russians have often sensed that improvement would require precisely those traits that they disdain in us. A dose of American practical energy and blind optimism, for example, might go a long way to dissipating the country's besetting lethargy. The more change seems necessary, the more have Americans seemed worth copying. Even Stalin occasionally turned in our direction when he needed an inspirational symbol. "American efficiency," he announced in 1931, "is that indomitable force which neither knows nor recognizes obstacles, which continues at a task once started until it is finished, even if it is a minor task; and without which serious constructive work is impossible."

Recalling life in Moscow in the 1920s, Pitirim Sorokin (who later became a Harvard sociologist) remarked, "Whenever there appeared among us an unusually energetic, efficient, inventive and optimistic type he was nicknamed our 'Russian American.' " The juxtaposition of the two words disguises a psychological crisis. How could Russians model themselves on the pattern that they scorned? How could they become what they wanted to keep at arm's length? During communism's self-confident period, an easy solution seemed imminent. In building their new world, Russians would not copy Americans but would surpass them; capitalism would fall by the wayside, leaving Russians to be the new Americans of the modern age. "I realized that even I, a dissipated bohemian poet," thundered Mayakovsky, in the poem "100%," "was much more like this [ideal] American fellow than the real American of today; there are no such 'guys' today."

With *perestroika* teetering, a Russian-American seems to be required more urgently than ever, but there is little confidence that the transmogrification can be carried out as simply as Mayakovsky believed. Russians consider the impending operation tentatively, almost plaintively. I remembered a comment by Peter Zverlov, the director at Dialog, the Russian-American joint venture. He had insisted that Russian brainpower, as much as American organizational skill, would lead to business success. At the time it seemed to be a remark only about the division of labor, but I think it was also meant as a sort of anatomical schema, a marking of a Russian essence that would always endure, he hoped.

Over the years Russians have developed a moral strategy for dealing with the problems the American character presents to them. In this analysis of the American character, mention of specific traits is largely avoided in favor of a focus on our essential being, the core underlying all traits. It's striking how this perspective resolves many of the embarrassments and tensions that are otherwise so troubling.

What is really most peculiar about Americans, goes this argument, is our willingness to invent ourselves as we go along, to assume whatever traits and in whatever measure that the circumstances require. Our character has the remarkable capacity to be fluid, protean, endlessly adaptive; we have been pragmatic and energetic and risk-taking not because these traits inhere in us but because our history has required it. This belief dates back at least to the nineteenth century. Alexander Lakier, whose *Travels Through North America, Canada and Cuba* (1856) is the first extended eyewitness report about America by a Russian, was struck by many things he saw, but most of all by the kaleidoscopic character of the inhabitants. In a typical passage he wrote, "The American does not become attached to any one occupation: today a farmer, tomorrow an official, then a merchant and a seafarer. This is not because he is fickle but because he is adroit enough to accommodate himself to any occupation he chooses. He will finally settle on the one that is most lucrative." Russians admit that fluidity of character, the ability to fit to any occupation, makes for a highly efficient society; but at what cost?

The poet Alexander Pushkin, considering America in 1835, offered an answer to this question that has found many echoes through the years: ". . . with astonishment we have seen democracy in its repulsive cynicism, in its cruel prejudices and in its unendurable tyranny." In America, public opinion held sway because no one had any inner purpose, no morality based on self-understanding; everyone adapted the guise that was socially convenient: "On the part of those governing, timidity and servility; the man of talent, out of respect for equality, [is] forced to voluntary ostracism; the rich man [puts] on a tattered caftan, so that on the street he will not offend proud beggary, which he secretly condemns." Because their personality is so fluid, so adaptable, Americans are unprincipled, drifting with every passing current. Americans may sometimes be good, but as easily can be bad. There is no constraint, no inner boundary to keep us from enacting our whims.

Russians believe their psychology follows different laws. In 1870, a Russian military mission that had come to Connecticut to inspect a newly invented rifle was nonplussed to learn that the designer, General Hiram Berdan, took equal pride in being a candy maker. In Russia, only an eccentric had interests that divergent. One is what one is; you must be true to your essence. Such fatalism has always been reinforced by politics—in tsarist times, if you were born a peasant you stayed a peasant, born a merchant you stayed a merchant, and after the Revolution, Party discipline accomplished much the same ends. But the national psychology also has a lot to do with it. To the natives, almost without exception, "the Russian soul" is not a mythical creature. It is that elegantly formed, well-grounded entity that lives within each Russian, setting the limits to life's experiences. You may wrestle with God and cry to heaven (as characters in those famous Russian novels do), but you cannot change who you are—even though you might end up changing the world around you. There is an old Russian folk saying, "Living your life is not taking a stroll across a field," that suggests the burden of self each Russian must carry with him. How different are Americans, who seem to move with no moral anchor, always adopting the course that will get them most easily around life's complexities.

I have a friend who is an editor at *SShA (USA)*, the publication of the Institute of the United States and Canada. Long exposure to the topic has made him canny about Americans. He said to me, "You want to know the difference between Russians and Americans? I will tell you. If a Russian finds a stray dog on the street, he will as soon sell it to some butcher for dog meat as take it into his home—but if he does take it home he will care for the dog till the day it dies. If an American finds a dog he will certainly take it home, no question about it. But then! He will nurture it for a month, perhaps two, and end by giving it up to the dog pound for extermination without a second thought."

My friend says he likes Americans, and indeed he told his anecdote in a way that suggested he found our sudden impulses endearing. But I didn't ask him how he would rate our behavior on a scale of moral values. In fact, I didn't say anything. We were sitting in the Café Pirosmani, a privately operated restaurant near the Novo Devichy cemetery. Most of these restaurants are tourist traps. They overcharge unconscionably and don't give much in return except a hint of posh and a fighting chance to beat the usual hour-between-each-course service. But my friend knew the restaurant owner, as he seemed to know everyone in Moscow, and so we got special treatment. The food and drink had been excellent, the service gracious, and our conversation lively. But his little anecdote brought the good cheer to a dead stop.

In France or Germany or England, the issue of my nationality rarely is a problem. There are plenty of people in those countries who do not like Americans, but it's easy to spot them and stay out of their way. In Russia, it's trickier. The habit of seeing Americans as both similar and different causes sparks when you least expect it. Even the happiest occasions, like my dinner at the Café Pirosmani, can slip quietly but implacably toward misunderstanding.

Despite all of their carping, Russians insist that they like Americans, preferring us to all other foreigners. You find this opinion everywhere, in the off-the-cuff comments of strangers and in well-reasoned editorials, on the street and in domestic circles—Americans are amiable, friendly, wonderfully congenial. The prevalence of this view makes it hard to resist, but I think it has to be qualified. When Russians say they like Americans, they have in mind a particular kind of American.

One way to get a sense of what Russians prefer in our national character is by noting the individuals they have designated as authentic American heroes. What qualifies an American for the pantheon that Russians have devised for us? Benjamin Franklin, one of the earliest nominees, acted (or seemed to act) with simplicity and candor; the title of the translated version of *Poor Richard's Almanac* was *Uchenie dobrodushnogo Rikarda (The Teachings of Goodhearted Richard)*, an alteration that helped to emphasize the Franklin that most appealed to Russians. Henry Ford, another of their heroes, was celebrated for his technological genius but also because of his straight-talking style. Thomas Edison had the simplicity and directness Russians prize in us; the standard Soviet biography of him is almost embarrassingly adoring.

Canniness in an American is often perceived as no more than low cunning. A bluff and eager openness to life is our preeminent national virtue. Because Russians saw such qualities in the lives of Jack London and Ernest Hemingway, they admired their fiction all the more; Hemingway's photo was in the home of numerous Moscow intellectuals in the 1960s, an homage as much to his adventuresome spirit as to his fiction. By contrast, even when Edgar Allan Poe enjoyed great popularity, his dark brooding was considered against the American grain. One critic declared Poe not really an American at all, but an aristocrat, "a spiritual son of Oxford." Too much introspection in an American is not only bad for the soul but sufficient grounds, apparently, for revocation of citizenship.

The American braggart is a figure that Russians scorn, but they draw a fine line. They admire American cockiness and self-assurance. This distinction is elusive, but Russians have a benchmark for their judgments—the quality of reticence marks the true American hero. It constitutes proof of an inner strength that feels no need to advertise itself. It is instructive, in this regard, to compare the Russian reputations of heavyweight champions Joe Louis and Muhammad Ali. Louis, who was famous for his unassuming bearing outside the ring and his ferocity in it, was defined by the newspaper *Red Sport* as "the worthy son of the American people." Though Ali was respected for his stand against the Vietnam War, he was too self-aware and self-dramatizing to gain unreserved affection. "Despite his outward extravagance, Ali made a very good impression on our boys," *Pravda* noted during the 1969 American tour by Soviet boxers. The qualifying clause is a judgment; "outward extravagance" distances an American from his best virtues.

Even American political leaders, who normally call forth little affection, can be redeemed by straightforwardness of character. Woodrow Wilson, who was disliked for permitting the Allied Expeditionary Force to invade Soviet soil, was even more scorned because of his personality; cartoonists of the day caricatured him as a bespectacled intellectual hiding behind the gobbledygook of learning, and Mayakovsky, with his gift for the telling pejorative, denounced him (in the poem "150,000") as "fat"—wildly inaccurate as physical description, the epithet was of a piece with the Russian dislike of Americans who seemed smug, complacent, self-centered. By contrast, Franklin Roosevelt and John Kennedy were admired even though they promoted policies inimical to Soviet interests. Unfriendly actions were redeemed by plain speaking and, in Kennedy's case, an appearance of youthful spontaneity. The political leader who over the years has been most admired is probably Abraham Lincoln. When he died, demonstrations of grief in Russia were widespread, and the eulogies went beyond official lip service. Leo Tolstoy explained the affection for the assassinated president: "[Lincoln] was one who wanted to be great through his smallness." That is still the trait that counts the most. The ability to stay close to the bone, to disregard pomp, is perceived as an American value of high order.

This being the Soviet Union, it is impossible that ideology not play a role in determining which Americans make it onto the roll call of heroes. It was no accident that Walt Whitman, who enjoyed great popularity in the early days of communism, wrote poems that could be distributed as morale builders to Baku oil workers in the 1920s. But if politics is often a factor in the Russian perspective on Americans, the logic is never lockstep. Though there has been a lot of official praise for Americans with leftist politics, genuine admiration is reserved for those who fit a particular psychological profile, who behave in a particular way. Whitman was perceived to fit these more stringent personal specifications as well as political ones. He was a man of "unafraid thoughts and unafraid actions," said Anatoly Lunacharsky, the Soviet minister of education, and it was this that guaranteed high esteem in Russia. He was, indeed, popular even before the Revolution gave its ideological blessings. On the other hand, Mark Twain was admired even after he offended socialist sensibilities by his actions during the Gorky Affair. (Gorky was vilified by the New York press for sharing a hotel room with a woman who was not his wife, whereupon most of his American sponsors—including Twain—deserted him and ran for cover.) Russians liked Twain for his directness before this sorry episode, and they continued to like him for it afterward.

Perhaps the best example of an American's manner overriding his politics is that of Theodore Dreiser, who was rabidly anti-communist when he visited the Soviet Union in 1931. To Soviet eyes, Dreiser's politics were not only reprehensible in their principles but downright irritating in their application. He refused to credit any progress the Soviets claimed to have made, mocking everything with a coy knowingness. "I watched a parade today. Why did all those people march? . . . were they really as enthusiastic as they seemed?" he inquired. He was a master at baiting his hosts. Seeing worshipers hurrying into a church and ignoring the sign—"Religion is the opium of the people"—which the authorities had affixed near the entrance, he heartily declared, "They seem to be taking their opium." But a directness, an impatience with cant, showed through the Dreiser style and made up for his nonstop hectoring. He was received warmly, and made many friends. Meeting Nikolai Bukharin, the Party's chief theoretician, Dreiser taunted him about the regime's divergences from Marxism, pressing him to admit that class divisions still existed in the workers' state. "My God, take him away!" Bukharin exclaimed. "I can't stand any more." But he nevertheless seems to have found Dreiser congenial.

Indeed, once Russians have located their favorite American, it takes a lot to shake their faith. Their descriptions can assume a worshipful tone, an embarrassing laudatory style that seeks to turn every mundane detail into a relic. The American's every word and gesture is made to seem an expression of distaste for dissembling and pomposity. The painter Andrew Wyeth is one who has been treated as an icon of American virtues, and a Soviet visitor's report of his visit to Wyeth's home has all the telltale marks of this special hagiographic genre, right down to props attesting to a love of simple manual labor. "He greeted us with a toss of his head, not releasing the stack of firewood he held in his hands," we are told. Even the physical setting seems charged with simple values. "This was not a modish house, remodeled and decorated 'in the old style,' but genuine oldness, magnificent and touched by time." The depiction transforms Wyeth into a paragon of simplicity. It is certain, indeed, that Wyeth's hugely popular 1987 exhibition at the Pushkin Museum in Moscow was a celebration of his personality as much as of his paintings.

It must be said that the Russian pantheon of American heroes comprises an unsurprising list. After all, these same individuals are held up as models by Americans themselves. But the Russian selections are guided by a special reasoning—the reward for living up to the virtues of simplicity that our best men exemplify is, so their argument goes, better understanding between our two nations. They roll out the evidence to make their case. Isn't it true that of all peoples Russians and Americans go over on a first-name basis most quickly? Aren't we by national temperament equally eager to escape the suffocating politesse and social conventions that constrain sincerity? Isn't it true that there have been moments of affection so elemental that even language was unnecessary—for example, all those intermarriages, with American soldiers stationed in Moscow during World War II, with academics on exchange programs in the years after, where simple, intense feelings overcame all obstacles? Following the curve of the heart, we could be friends, exuberant companions, lovers.

They've enshrined this belief in their films, including the very first Soviet film with an American character, Lev Kuleshov's *The Extraordinary Adventures of Mr. West in the Land of the Bolsheviks* (1924). Mr. West, an American businessman, decides to travel to the Soviet Union despite the advice of friends and relatives. He is curious about the new world that communism has created. Kuleshov provides Mr. West with a beaverskin coat to wear and a cowboy for a bodyguard, adornments meant to mark him as American, as does his expression of perpetual surprise. Arriving in Moscow, he naively allows his briefcase to be stolen and then manages to get himself kidnapped. But the culprits, contrary to his expectations, are not the Bolsheviks but a gang of counterrevolutionaries. The Bolsheviks rescue Mr. West from the clutches of the evildoers. The final scene is a celebratory tour through Moscow with Mr. West rollicking in the backseat of a convertible with a bluff and friendly commissar beside him.

Made some forty years later, the film *Peace to the Newborn* (1962) portrays Americans with much the same condescending affection. During the final battle of Germany in World War II, a Red Army soldier who is cut off from his unit stumbles upon a woman on the verge of giving birth. Desperate for help, the Soviet soldier finds an American corporal repairing his truck. The American is drunk, foolhardy, and lascivious—at the mention of a woman he winks knowingly. But when he learns that a baby's life is at stake, the American jumps into the truck, guns the engine as he slashes through a German roadblock, and delivers the group to a Soviet hospital. The final scene is of the American awkwardly joining a rambunctious cossack dance with Red Army nurses.

*Mr. West* was made when official policy toward America was not implacably hostile and occasionally even tentatively friendly, but by the time of *Peace to the Newborn,* America was an ideological foe. The American character apparently has virtues that can transcend American politics. Neither the businessman nor the corporal is perfect—when they first appear both behave with dubious morality. But they are ultimately redeemed by their simplicity. The basic instincts of the two Americans are good, and as these are allowed to emerge the men become more attractive; it's no accident that the two films end with scenes of exuberant physicality, displays of affection on the level of sheer movement. When Americans are natural, they are good. And when they are good, they get along wonderfully well with Russians.

It's the glitter and pomp, the grasping after false idols, that keep

Americans from their best natures. Strip away the trappings of our distracting and trivial life, the Russians say, and we and they would find common ground. This belief is so strong that even commissars and bureaucrats have occasionally been seduced. There would seem to be few less promising situations than the writer Konstantin Simonov visiting Hollywood, the communist ideologue in the belly of the capitalist beast; but the ideal of simplicity was made to triumph even here. During Simonov's visit in 1947, there was much he despised, but he found some happy moments with new friends, particularly Charlie Chaplin, John Garfield, and the director Lewis Milestone. Before departing he wanted to thank them for their kindnesses. He decided against presents or souvenirs. Instead he invited them and their wives to what might be called a Ceremony of Simplicity (*prosto-naprosto* as he put it, "simplicity at its simplest"). Comandeering for the evening a rusty old Soviet freighter that happened to be in port, Simonov concocted a dinner of the most basic, most purely human elements. The table was set in the captain's sparsely furnished cabin. The *bufetchitsa* (barmaid) Masha, a "tall stout woman with traces of lost beauty," greeted the guests "like a hostess in her own home," all the while whispering the traditional Russian words of welcome, *"milosti prosim."* Everyone was made to eat a full ration of borscht and to drink vodka. According to Simonov, Chaplin was especially taken by Masha's earthy commentary on his films; he liked her "natural independence and inner sense of equality." Everyone was somehow strengthened to go back out into the Hollywood world of rumor-mongering and money-grubbing. For a space of time, anyway, these Americans had been given the opportunity to show their best side.

Russians sometimes seem to be determined to find their simple, instinctual American no matter what the obstacles. They embrace us in bear hugs, envelop us in their exuberance, establish elemental contact—even as we remonstrate that there must be some mistake. Over the centuries, the basic plot has always been Russians rambunctiously advancing, Americans shrinking back, fending off politely. While on his goodwill tour of Russia in 1862, Undersecretary of the Navy Gustavus Fox noted, "All Americans were treated to a peculiarly Russian custom—a tossing in the air at the hands of the host. The sensation is anything but pleasant." Almost a century later, on V-E Day, chargé d'affaires George Kennan hid in the corridors of the American embassy to avoid a similar fate. In the interval between those two encounters, and afterward as well, numberless Americans have been subjected to similar demonstrations of a heartiness that is intended to prove we are really brothers under the skin of our nationalities.

It's this sort of thing that makes me a bit nervous whenever I have gone to a party in Russia where I don't know the other guests. The evening can easily turn into a celebration of Russian-American friendship, with me the main stage prop. At first there will be a general tentativeness, as I am sized up for any resistant qualities. Later, once the party starts warming up, everyone will tell jokes about the American character, and I'll be expected to add my bit to the fun. At some point the drinking will begin in earnest, and that's when danger lurks. This is the moment when Americans are expected to prove our congeniality. We must make contact on the simplest of human levels, when we are too drunk to think too much—semiconscious amiability being taken as the best proof that the national characters of our two countries are indeed alike. I've tried pleading headaches, or setting some reasonable limits to consumption beforehand, or announcing in advance that I will be leaving early. The Russians smile sympathetically and nod in assent, but when the party spirit overtakes them, they become possessed, refusing to heed any objection or excuse. If an American doesn't match them drink for drink, they are not only disappointed but insulted that we've rejected their advice about what is best for us. We've denied our best instincts. I cherish many of the evenings I've spent with Russians who are close friends—but I can do without those semiofficial celebrations of the simple American nature.

"American humor is a bit coarse, a bit childish, but I like it all the same," I was told by Boris Pyanov, the editor-in-chief of *Kro-*

*kodil.* "Listen, I will tell you the quintessential American joke, the joke that most reveals the American character." I had been sitting in his office for about fifteen minutes by then. Our encounter had begun on a high note, with his proclamation that Russians and Americans have much in common, and that his recent trip to the United States had convinced him our nations could be fast friends. But after that, things had gone downhill with alarming speed. With his sad, basset-hound look and lugubrious manner, Pyanov did not fit the image of a man who was supposed to know how to make people laugh. He spoke in the measured tones of a diplomat conducting negotiations, and our conversation was almost ready to expire from lack of air.

I had pressed him on several points, asking in particular for examples of the naïveté he claimed to have found among American college students. He became annoyed that I had challenged him, and dismissed my query as inane. When I said a longer trip might have led him to other conclusions, he gave me a sharp look. We seemed to have taken a dislike to each other though we had just met. I interpreted his offer to tell the joke as a last-ditch effort at sociability, and prepared to do my part by responding with signs of merriment.

"Here it is, then," he said. "A young man has an accident and has to go to the hospital. Despite all the doctor's efforts, it is necessary to amputate his leg. The next day the man's father visits the hospital to comfort his son. But then, when the father offers some words of kindness, the son laughs and replies, 'That's all right, this way there are fewer places for the mosquitoes to bite me.'"

Uttering the punch line, Pyanov settled back in his chair to await my laugh. But, despite my best intentions, I hesitated. His preamble, promising to reveal the essence of the American character, had raised the stakes, making his joke also an assertion of knowledge. It was, I suppose, not impossible to interpret the joke as another instance of Russian admiration for American simplicity, for our sunny optimism and unstoppable good cheer; but sitting there with

Pyanov's cool stare upon me, I found it hard to do that. Rather the joke seemed a contentious maneuver, a ploy to gain the high ground. To call someone else simple is simultaneously to make a claim for one's own encompassing wisdom, broad enough, at least, to recognize mere simplicity. I did not laugh at Pyanov's joke, and we parted on a strained note.

Was I too hard on Pyanov, too suspicious of his intentions? Since relations between our countries have been so strained, isn't it best to give the benefit of the doubt when a Russian announces his congeniality? I probably had been a bit ungracious, I decided, but I cheered myself up with the thought that I had been pushed in that direction. In official and semi-official encounters (though rarely, thank God, in personal ones), Russians treat Americans with a bonhomie so hearty it is suspicious. The proofs they display to show how much we delight them—that joke of Pyanov's, for example—often turn out to be disturbingly double-edged. When they praise us for our simplicity, they may simultaneously be mocking us as fools.

It is to the point, therefore, to recall one more American here who has caught Russians' attention. Benjamin Franklin and JFK, Joe Louis and Henry Ford—if the Russian roll call of American heroes is a tribute to our directness and our dislike of pomp, then John Paul Jones should be included as a reminder that these same traits are ones that Russians sometimes exploit. Jones should probably have an asterisk next to his name, since he was born a Scotsman; but it was his feats with the American colonial navy during the American Revolution that caught Catherine the Great's eye and began an episode that might rightly be entitled "The American Hero Brought Low in Russia." Catherine, battling Turkey for control of the Black Sea and handicapped by a lack of trained naval officers, offered Jones the rank of *kontradmiral* in the Imperial Navy. Jones accepted and took command of his squadron with high hopes. But things went disastrously wrong fairly quickly.

Upon arriving at his post, Jones found that Georgi Potemkin, the Russian commander-in-chief and Catherine's personal favorite, meant to shunt him aside in favor of his own protégé. Bewildered by court intrigues and innocent about lines of influence, Jones found himself isolated and fighting off slander. After one engagement he was charged with timidity; subsequently, after a brilliant victory, the honors due to him were given to another. Seeking to justify himself, Jones wrote an emotional letter to Catherine, but the only result was that Potemkin, angered by the circumvention, relieved him of his command. Jones was forced to depart his flagship in an open galley. The journey took three days and nights, and Jones contracted pneumonia.

The *kontradmiral* settled in St. Petersburg with the intention of persuading the empress to give him back his command, but his situation only got worse. In April 1789, it was reported by the chief of police that Jones had attempted to rape a ten-year-old girl. According to the police account, the girl was peddling butter when Jones's lackey led her into the apartment, where the master locked the door, knocked the girl out with a blow to the chin, and assaulted her. There was an affidavit from an army surgeon attesting to the rape.

Jones at first insisted nothing had happened. The girl had come to him of her own volition, asking if he had lace to mend. "She then indulged in some rather lively and indecent gestures. I advised her not to enter upon so vile a career, gave her some money; and dismissed her." But at other times, Jones offered a more incriminating version of what happened. "The accusation [of rape] against me is an imposture invented by the mother of one *fille perdue* who came several times to my house and with whom I have often bandined [*sic*], always giving her money, but whose virginity I have definitely not taken. . . ."

Jones's main line of defense was that he was being framed, and as the investigation proceeded his contention seems to have been borne out. The mother admitted that her daughter was far from innocent, having been seduced by Jones's lackey three months before, and that she had continued calmly to peddle butter after the alleged rape. The mother hinted she had been put up to the whole thing by "a gentleman who wore the star of some order," which suggests that someone was determined that Jones not regain his influence with the empress.

But these revelations did not help Jones much. The scandal had gone too far, and Jones had not helped his case with his varying accounts of what had happened. He was dropped totally by Petersburg society. In June 1789, he was permitted to kiss the hand of the empress at public audience and given a *bon voyage*—chewed up and spit out by a sophisticated milieu he utterly failed to understand, a simple American hero destroyed by Russian worldliness.

Carol Burnett appears in my hotel room—that is, she appears on the television screen, but her manner is so intimate that it makes her presence seem palpable. She is giving an interview before the showing of a movie in which she stars, and she seems more realistically worn than I remember from Stateside television. Perhaps she has suffered through an uncomfortable flight or perhaps Soviet makeup techniques are not up to ours; more likely, it is what she was saying. Carol (her manner invites a first-name familiarity) states that she has a deep interest in the movie because its topic is alcoholism. Her own parents were alcoholics. Her daughter, who sits demurely at her side, is a recovered alcoholic. In the States, such a confession would be old hat, just the stuff our media mills routinely spin out; here it is like a thunderclap in a cloudless sky. Russians have plenty of problems with alcohol, but they don't broadcast them if they can help it.

Public expression here is in general carefully circumscribed. Rules of conduct, which are partly the vestige of the formalities of the tsarist period and partly the effect of communism's social engineering, demand the suppression of intimacies in front of strangers. Citizens do not proclaim their fantasies and dreams; they hide them, or hoard them for a more favorable moment, or just forget about them. Behavior on the streets of Russian cities is testimony to the prevailing reticence. Lovers do not kiss, children do not shout, teenagers do not blare their radios, and even drunks are quiet drunks. Smiles are the exception, Russians preferring to go about their business with uniformly dour expression; they will laugh once they get home to family and friends. Dress adheres to a determinedly modest code. Any unusual attire draws looks and comment. Once, exiting my hotel for a morning's run in my jogging shorts, I was stopped by the porter: *"Molodoy chelovek, u nas v trusikakh ne khodyat* (Young man, we do not go around in our underpants here)." The public collective moves in a stately and decorous fashion more appropriate to a nineteenth-century middle-European kingdom than to the playground of successful revolutionaries.

That finally may be the biggest difference between the American and Russian national character—not the particular traits each possesses, but how and in what forum these are made visible. The American habit of parading personal detail startles Russians. Our fascination with intimacies is more than bad taste; it suggests an utterly alien way of looking at life. American newspapers (which of course operate at a slightly brasher pitch than our society in general), have often provided Russians with all the evidence they need to prove our puerile curiosity. After enduring questions from an American journalist about when he went to bed and what he ate for breakfast, Leo Tolstoy pronounced the newspaper's readership "feebleminded." Some sixty years later, in 1931, Americans' interest in the domestic routines of others was unabated. During a shipboard press conference, the visiting writer Boris Pilnyak was interrogated about his choice of tie and shoes and the precise color of his hair. ("I have, it turns out, sandy hair," he ironically noted in the memoir of his trip.) Pilnyak claimed the ordeal was like being "poked at," but both he and Tolstoy were shielded by a protective arrogance; Peter Tchaikovsky presented a more sensitive target. After reading a review of his New York conducting debut, Tchaikovsky noted in his diary, "This is what I read in *The Herald:* 'Tchaikovsky is a tall, gray, well-built, interesting man, well on to sixty. He seems a trifle embarrassed and responds to the applause by a succession of brusque and jerky bows.' . . . It angers me that they write not only about my music but about my person too." Tchaikovsky was high-strung but not so much that his reaction was merely idiosyncratic. Americans, most Russians believe, intrude into areas which should be off-limits, or open only to intimates of long standing.

Over the years, Russians have grown somewhat more accustomed to Americans' blithe trespasses. They now are on their guard, wary. Many diplomats and artists and others who deal regularly with Americans have developed a style that deflects curiosity—a sort of ironic bonhomie. But there is always room for surprise; America, it seems, can always screw up its inquisitiveness a notch or two more. When the novelist Vasily Aksyonov lectured at UCLA in 1970, he was regarded as one of the canniest observers of American ways (his fiction was famous for its "American style"), but even he got knocked for a loop by our manners. A student rose from the audience to ask a question—though not, as it turned out, about the lecture topic. Were Aksyonov's pants, she wanted to know, the sort of thing that Russians habitually wore? It takes more than a general awareness of Americans' odd habits to get through this kind of encounter; one must possess some ingrained and automatic resistance to social embarrassment, such as Carol Burnett seemed to have.

A few days after the Burnett interview, I got a chance to see at firsthand what might happen if her sort of confessional style were carried over into Russian life. I was invited to a meeting of the first Alcoholics Anonymous group in the Soviet Union. In its belief that public acknowledgment of flaws is a way to self-improvement, A.A. is peculiarly American. How could it fit into the Russian way of doing things? If a Russian decides that his drinking has reached a point where it interferes with his daily rounds, he may have a chat with his friend. But he would not characterize the issue as a "drinking problem"—life cannot so easily be stuffed into categories—and still less would he think to discuss it with a group of strangers. Nevertheless, the representative from A.A. was optimistic. He told me that Raisa Gorbachev was so impressed by the A.A. approach that she wondered if it might not be a good idea to form a few Overeaters Anonymous chapters also. This was even harder for me to imagine. I could not picture Russians, who are world-class trenchermen, sitting around a table and analyzing their weaknesses for borscht and piroshki.

The A.A. meeting was held in the Babushkin section of the city, which abuts the railroad yards. The streets, the buildings, even the passersby seemed especially forlorn. No one I asked could help me to find the address I had scribbled on a slip of paper; they seemed stymied by a neighborhood so nondescript it lacked all landmarks. After much difficulty, I homed in on a dark courtyard of five-story buildings, each with a lone naked light bulb marking its entrance. No house numbers were visible, and I asked a young man sitting on one of the stoops for directions; he only shrugged his shoulders. Down the block I could make out the harsh bluish light of a *gastronom* (provisions store), presumably with the usual long queues and the usual empty bins. It was all pretty dreary. If you didn't drink before, life in such a setting would make you seriously consider the option.

The apartment, when I finally found it, was three small rooms. In one of these, nine people sat around a large table, with a few more in chairs against the walls. It was a varied group, ranging from a man of about fifty, carefully dressed and with the look of a bureaucrat, to a couple of laborers still in their work clothes. There were three women, all in their thirties. The A.A. representative, who sat at one end of the table, wore a tan vest and a green bow tie that somehow implied optimism. Speaking through an interpreter, he opened the meeting by asking if anyone wanted to relate any recent experiences.

"My name is Volodya. I am an alcoholic." This is A.A.'s prescribed formula for beginning to speak, but it sounded odd in Russian, and especially from this all-too-Russian speaker, a gangly fellow with a mustache and an ill-fitting suit. He looked just off the farm, hardly a candidate for self-awareness through public confession. But he told his story with competence. Yesterday, he had gone around to a friend's house to help repair the bathroom sink, a task which took most of the afternoon. When it was finally finished, the friend wanted to thank him in the traditional Russian way—a couple of belts of vodka. "I knew he would be insulted if I said no," Volodya commented, "but I held firm. Water is not so bad when you realize what is at stake." He sat down to a round of polite applause.

The A.A. representative commented on Volodya's remarks, pausing between phrases to give the translator time to do her job. "Remember this rule: do not think of sobriety in terms of a lifetime. Do not think in terms even of weeks. Get through one day at a time. Each day make a list of things you can be grateful for. Yes, write it down. Always begin with this item: 'today I am sober.' Read it aloud to yourself if you feel it will make more of an impression. 'Today I am sober.' "

Volodya stared so intently at the A.A. representative that it seemed he was trying to get a physical grip on the words—and indeed, I thought to myself, the advice had a pragmatic air that must have appeared utterly foreign. Telling intimate stories in public was odd enough; being told to work a transformation of the spirit by following a schedule contradicted all Russian common sense.

Another speaker began her tale. It was far more bitter. Her brother had called to announce he was coming home after a three-day spree with friends, and that his mother had better have a bottle of vodka ready for his arrival. He had no time to waste queuing up at the local store. In a sad but strangely placid tone, the woman told the group that she was worried about the violence her brother might do; but she was also worried that she might attempt to smooth over any argument by joining her brother in a drink.

"Think of yourself first," the A.A. representative said. "Nothing you do is as important as keeping your own sobriety. Not your friends, not even your family."

Like the first speaker, the woman responded with stolid surprise to the advice, a reaction that made sense to me. For Russians the family is sacrosanct, even when its members are at each other's throats. Can you simply throw over this tradition in the name of some newfangled theory of self-improvement?

After a few more equally woeful statements from the floor followed by similarly practical advice, the A.A. representative offered a summarizing statement. A practiced speaker, he gauged his audience. He paused for an extra beat to increase the anticipation. Then he said, "I've done many interesting things in my life. But nothing has been as interesting as sitting here tonight."

After pausing again, he said, "I have met many people whose company I have enjoyed. But it's been nothing compared to the pleasure I have in being with the people in this room tonight."

Another pause. "I have been to many marvelous places in my life. But no place has been as marvelous as this room."

This time the pause was so extended that his last words seemed to hang in the air, inviting everyone to examine them. And this struck me as very risky. The A.A. representative meant to lend importance to this little gathering of desperate Russians, but if you thought too long his words could reveal their other aspect. His reference to the great world beyond, the world that Americans routinely visit and where they routinely find excitement, made this small apartment with its window looking out on a dreary courtyard even more depressing. Inadvertently, the A.A. representative had pulled rank, the rank of his nationality. Some of the people, I noticed, moved uneasily in their chairs. The American motifs that had adorned this meeting, that advice about making lists and abjuring family ties and so on, now seemed not only foreign but intrusively foreign, an attack on native ways.

The A.A. representative finished his summary, and there was a short lull while everyone wondered what should follow. I bent over my notebook ready to transcribe the next comment; but I never got the chance. The translator had risen from her chair and without preamble was addressing me. All eyes turned in my direction. The change in my perspective was dizzying—from being a fly on the wall to a specimen under the microscope. The representative of the American press, as the translator grandly denominated me, should be sure to report honestly what he had seen. No distortion, just the facts. America should see Russia as it was, without embroidery or fancy theories. The words were polite, no more really than a true description of my activity, but the tone had a combative edge. I had been put in my place; though I meant to be in that place anyway, it made a difference to be put there, and the effect was to alter the psychological balance in the room. The evening was now something other than a long roll call of American definitions and prescriptions.

I became aware that the young man sitting on my left, who during the whole meeting had been silent and almost motionless, was fidgeting to his feet. Like a stone come to life, he began to speak. "I have listened as everyone says how grateful they are for the support they get from these meetings. I have at times said this myself. But do you want to know the truth? I am not grateful, not truly. What I am feeling is the opposite, that I wish you would leave me alone. That is the way I am." He subsided once more into his surly silence, virtually daring anyone to challenge him with kindness or optimism.

I realized how different this was from what had come before. Though there had been confession, there had been little anguish, narration but no crisis. The young man offered no events, no story with a plot, but only a picture of blank pain that could not be ameliorated. Life's problems run too deep, his attitude implied. His comment amounted to a declaration that America's remedies were of little use here.

The rest of the group seemed to sense that the young man's pose constituted a coda of sorts, not to be tampered with. After a few more perfunctory remarks, the meeting stood adjourned. All rose and joined hands for the prayer with which A.A. meetings always conclude. I started to move aside, but the men at my right and left took my arms and neatly incorporated me into the circle. Several of the others smiled encouragingly at me, and to my surprise I found myself mouthing the words about hopes for a better future. It was strategically wise, even if not sincere. Remaining aloof from the exuberant community might have been interpreted as a rejection of the cease-fire in the conflict of national styles that had finally been achieved.

Russians' reluctance to display intimate feelings in public has a long and definable lineage. Looked at from a particular angle, permitting history to assert its weight, the events in that dreary room in the Babushkin region could be seen as the last link in a centuries-long chain.

The most distant link was forged in 1088, when Tsar Alexei welcomed Christianity into Russia. The agents of the conversion were two monks from Thessaloníkï in Greece, and the Christianity they brought with them was the Eastern Orthodox version. This distinction was crucial. Russia came to conceive of itself as an alternative, usually a superior alternative, to European Catholicism. It would be the "Third Rome" that would correct the errors of the original. Russians believed so fervently in the doctrinal truth of Orthodoxy that it was a natural step to believe also that it promoted a superior form of society. Orthodoxy, Russians insisted, fostered a sense of the collective; Western religions splintered society into hierarchies. Because the Orthodox liturgy was in a language (Church Slavonic) close to the vernacular, the faithful at prayer could feel themselves an active part of a congregation. Because the ecclesiastical order included clergy who intermingled with the community they served, church authority seemed less distant and imposing. *Sobornost,* the peculiarly Russian belief in a society of equals bound by a common spirit, flowed directly from Orthodoxy.

After the Revolution, the church's role was drastically curtailed. But *sobornost* did not die; it only took another form. It has often been noted that in terms of Marxist economic theory, Russia in 1917 was the wrong country for a revolution. (The capitalist infrastructure which communism was supposed to appropriate when it seized power had not yet developed.) But Russia was the right place in terms of a Marxist philosophy that makes consciousness primarily a function of the existing collective life; individual choice is less a matter of psychology than of sociology. The Soviet *kollektiv* is *sobornost* with a communist slant. And indeed, in Soviet Russia, as it was in tsarist Russia, the judgment of others is crucial. The besetting anxiety is of transgressing the community's mores. That old cliché about the Russian character rings true in both pre- and postrevolutionary times: in the place in the psyche where Westerners have a sense of personal guilt, a Russian has a sense of social shame.

*Sobornost* allows for public confessions, but only of failures to conform to the standards of the collective; problems caused by one's personal demons do not fit onto the agenda. It might be said, therefore, that the skein of attitudes that began with Tsar Alexei's conversion finally enfolded that group in the Babushkin apartment, making for the awkwardness I had seen. But how—precisely—did history and tradition get into the act? Did Volodya, dressed up in a suit for perhaps the first time in his life, or any of the others in that room, really conceive of what was happening in such grand terms? Not one of them seemed much of a student of intellectual history. A nation's tradition, it is said, is in the bones of its citizens, but how much attention do people typically pay to their bones?

But the invigorating power of conflict seems to have done the trick. The Russian concept of public behavior—like most broad social concepts—defines itself in terms of opposition. Russians, when they are forced to think about it, like to believe that they behave in precisely those ways that others do not. *Sobornost* was, among other important things, not European, and the communist *kollektiv* is emphatically not capitalist individualism. Nothing rouses the spirit like the presence of alien principles. The Russians in that Babushkin apartment may have had other things in mind when they arrived, but when exposed to the tenets of A.A., they became fervid believers in *sobornost* and passionate collectivists.

That A.A. is specifically an American invention could only have helped to push them in that direction. America fits into the historical scheme as the perfect opposite. In the eyes of Russians we are individualism incarnate, and it does not much matter to them if this quality is traceable back to the pioneer sensibility or to the capitalist economic system. It is no accident that Dostoevsky, who was an ardent proponent of *sobornost,* directed some of his fiercest thunderbolts toward America. When a character in *Crime and Punishment* prepares to commit suicide, Dostoevsky has him announce that he is "off to America." Life in America—where there is absolutely no sense of communal values—*is* death, the death of the soul. Given the role American has been cast in, I probably should have been glad that all the Russian A.A. group made me do was hold hands in a circle and say a few words I didn't believe in.

# four

# The Lay of the Land

One of the most galling facts of Soviet life has always been the restriction on travel abroad. It was far worse than living in some small, remote nation untouched by history. The Soviet Union was an active player in world affairs, but its citizens were confined behind its borders. Russians were therefore at one and the same time very aware of the rest of the world and ignorant of it. America, especially, was like some never-never land, continually imagined and never perceived.

Even today, in the age of *glasnost,* the old obstacles sometimes remain. My friend, the editor of *SShA,* has studied America for twenty years. He knows more about Ralph Nader and American jazz of the thirties and U.S. corporate spending than I ever will. But his every effort to visit America has been blocked. The last time was only a few months ago. My friend was all packed to go; at three o'clock on the morning of his flight, his telephone rang and he was told his visa had been canceled. No further explanation. He is still hopeful he will be permitted passage, but for now America remains an elusive hypothesis, just beyond his grasp. The failure to get to America tantalizes him. "I just want to see it. Once." That's it: just to see, to fill in his ideas with images taken from life.

Political restrictions are in fact easing, but economics has taken up much of the slack. Currency regulations limit to about two hundred dollars the amount of money that can be taken abroad. If a Russian is not lucky enough to know someone who will put him up, he may as well stay home; his survival time in the cold sea of capitalism would be measurable in milliseconds. In any case, few Russians even consider traveling to America; it is too hard to imagine being a tourist in a country that was until recently beyond the pale. As things stand, most Russians will form their picture of America as they have always done—by relying on the reports of the few who have made the journey.

There is a powerful tradition of Russian travel writing about America, and it does more than just present the facts. It insinuates a right way of looking at the facts. Arriving in New York harbor in 1922, the poet Sergei Esenin exclaimed, "The smoke wafts forth something mysterious, as though behind all these buildings something so immense is going on that it takes your breath away." In its suggestion that America's facades hide another reality, this comment typifies the Russian traveler's perspective.

The surfaces of America are deceptive. America is not self-evident. It must be treated less as a country lying at a calculable latitude and longitude than as a puzzle. Travelers from other countries have reached similar conclusions, but Russians take it one step further: America is a puzzle that can be solved. It is that most satisfying sort of mystery—one that can be made to yield up its secrets. As Esenin proceeded through America, he became more and more confident in his perceptive powers. Eventually he was explaining everything from America's Negro culture to its industrial development. His final remarks were about the secondhandedness of American culture—"Europe [presumably including Russia] smokes and throws away the fag ends. America picks them up and makes something immense out of them"—and they show a weary knowledge very far removed from his original awe.

Suspicious of the spectacle America presents, Russians who visit this country often strike a combative pose. They will not be easily impressed, they will not be bamboozled. Landfall and the first few days thereafter, that moment when America suddenly looms up as hard fact, have little of the usual pleasures of making port at a journey's end. It marks the beginning of the arduous task of seeing things correctly. America must be shown up, or rather the real America must be made to show through. The more assertively America presents itself, the more Russians look askance. "Oh no you don't," they seem always to be saying. "You'll have to do better than that to fool me." The Statue of Liberty has often served Russians as a means to prove that America will not seduce them. This was especially true in the postrevolutionary period, when patriotic sensibilities were acute. Vladimir Mayakovsky pointedly noted that the statue's flowing gown concealed a jail for illegal immigrants; another writer, Boris Pilnyak, insisted that he had not seen the statue at all as his ship steamed into the harbor but had gazed off in another direction; the director Konstantin Stanislavsky, on tour with the Moscow Art Theater, declared that he was distracted at the critical moment by newspaper reporters asking silly questions. One way or another, Russians are determined not to succumb to the view America offers of itself.

Though this perspective is not essentially political, it fits Russia's traditional political requirements—a way of describing America's achievements without giving them credit. Capitalism may look good at first glance, but look further. Beneath America's commanding surfaces there is inhumanity, beneath pretty exteriors an ugliness. One only has to look hard enough. The official account of Nikita Khrushchev's visit to America noted, "When you gaze down from an airplane, you could easily see a palace but not a hut. From there you could mistake the mansion of a billionaire living in cold seclusion for a health center." The American landscape cannot be allowed to remain mute and sedate; it must be continually interrogated to give up its true meanings.

The strategy of demystification revealed some unpleasant truths about America, but indiscriminate application dissipated its effectiveness—somewhere along the line the mode of thought became only a reflex. That some things may be exactly as they first seem was an idea not to be entertained seriously. Every phenomenon had to be probed and dissected to find the skull beneath the skin. *Business America (Delovaya Amerika),* by Nikolai Smelyakov, assistant minister of foreign trade, had a tremendous influence in the early 1960s, selling in the hundreds of thousands. Along with tables of data, it implied a story—a detective tracking a tricky suspect. Smelyakov found deception all around him, ferreting out clues where none would have thought to look. "The street lights," he noted of New York, "have little effect, and in many places don't exist at all. . . . In this way two birds can be killed with one stone: in the first place, the city authorities can economize on electricity, and in the second place the illuminated advertisements become more effective, since they stand out better against a dark background and better entice the passerby into the stores." Though Smelyakov's point was usually to reveal political or economic deceits, he did not stop there. Armed with the power of insight, he ranged across the whole of American life, finding hidden meaning in the most innocent phenomenon. Remarking on the New York subway, Smelyakov noted, "Even the ads here have traces of carelessness. Why spend money on those [i.e., the city's subway riders] who can hardly make ends meet?" That's an unexpected but arguably correct comment on capitalism. Remarking on the many homes that had libraries within, Smelyakov noted that quite a few of these were only "a decorative inlay on the wall, depicting a bookshelf filled with inscribed book spines." That's the comment of someone unwilling to accept the facts that stare him in the face. The visible is never as interesting as the invisible.

The detectivelike approach to America had its most influential expression in *One-Story America* by Ilya Ilf and Evgeny Petrov. Sections of the authors' chronicle of their 1935 trip appeared in *Pravda* and the journal *Znamya,* and the book became a classic as soon as it was printed. It is still widely read, and almost every book, article, or television report that describes America includes a nod in the direction of Ilf and Petrov.

Arriving in New York City, Ilf and Petrov bought themselves a new Ford, found themselves a friendly guide—a General Electric engineer who had worked in Russia for twelve years—and mapped out the itinerary of their three-month tour. They drove north to Niagara Falls, then proceeded through the Plains States to Arizona and California and back through the South, covering twenty-five states in all. It was a journey of discovery, in the literal sense of removing the disguising surface of things. Everywhere, in the most humble details, Ilf and Petrov found clues pointing to an America that contradicted the one on public display. In one hotel they examined a Bible, with a table of contents "especially composed by the solicitous management" to allow guests quickly to find passages dealing with matters ranging from spiritual debt to family disputes; Ilf and Petrov noted that there was also an entry for "success in business," with the relevant pages especially worn from use. So much for America's claims to religious feeling. At a boxing match, Ilf and Petrov remarked on the booing of the spectators, which was constant no matter what was happening in the ring. "It seems [Americans] come to boxing and football matches not to look on, but to yell." So much for America's claims to an interest in sports. They will not be surprised by anything America can throw at them. They don't even stop at making themselves the butt of a joke if it will puncture American pretensions. Buying the Ford puts them into an expansive mood, but in the next moment they skewer the false elation of American consumerism. "We were puffed with satisfaction at having managed to pick out the very best automobile out of the twenty-five million automobiles in America."

Even a small-town drugstore in upstate New York provided excellent material for demystification. The episode, Ilf and Petrov note, "might be entitled 'Pharmacist Without Mysticism, or The Secret of the American Drugstore.'" Once, they maintain, the American pharmacist was a man of genuine mystery, working behind a partition to grind out medicine "with his pestles in those thick china mortars." But by the time of their visit, all drugstores had come under the control of big business, which realized that it was more profitable to have medicines mass-produced beforehand. "There is not one drugstore left in New York where the pharmacist himself prepares medicines." Nevertheless, America tries to preserve the old sense of mystery. "Oh, this remarkable establishment wrapped in the aureole of medical mysteries! To prove that here medicines are actually prepared by hand the proprietor of the drugstore displays in the window a pile of yellowed old prescriptions. It all looks like the den of a medieval alchemist." That is America in a nutshell—all facade and extravagant posturing, which the discerning Russian eye should be able to penetrate.

This belief largely accounts for the tone of *One-Story America,* a jauntiness full of sly humor, suggesting that everything about America, even its seeming mysteries, is a good joke. Their trip, necessarily, had few surprises. "What traveler," they ask, "has not experienced that first and unrepeatable feeling of excited expectation that possesses the soul upon entering a city where he has never been before? . . . Nothing of that kind can be said about American cities. . . . almost all American cities resemble each other like the Canadian quintuplets, whom even their tender mother mistakes for each other. This colorless and depersonalized gathering of brick, asphalt, automobile, and billboards evokes in the traveler only a sense of annoyance and disappointment." Tourists from many countries have similarly found America clichéd and pedestrian; the singularity of Ilf and Petrov's response is the strain it seems to entail. They have achieved a position from where they command superior insight, and they will not be dislodged.

Their itinerary, purportedly sparked by wanderlust, turns out to be guided by imperatives that we can now see are recognizably Russian. America has to be dismantled, its wonders debunked. Visiting places that have awed the most jaded traveler, Ilf and Petrov are nonchalant. Though Niagara Falls is early on announced as the goal of the first leg of their trip, the sight merits only one sentence of dismissive irony. (Niagara's water has not yet, Ilf and Petrov remark, been packaged and marketed as "a benefit to the thyroid gland" or an aid to the consummation of "successful deals on the stock exchange.") They visit Hannibal, Missouri, but hardly notice the Mississippi except to remark on a cozy familiarity. ("The ascents and the slopes [down to the river] were as in a small town along the Volga." Almost everywhere they managed to uncover aspects of triviality, tastelessness, profiteering. Their motive was only partly political antagonism, and certainly not of the rabid sort. (Some Soviet critics found *One-Story America* too lenient by half.) They wanted to make America comprehensible.

In Sequoia National Park they consider one of the huge trees. "Near [the tree] hangs a little sign which with the greatest precision informs you that out of one such tree it is possible to build no less than forty-five houses and that, if you were to lay that tree beside a Union Pacific train, it would be longer than the train. But, looking at this tree, looking at all this transparent yet dark forest, we did not want to think of five-room houses and of Union Pacific trains." But that seems to be precisely what they did want to think about. The park was huge, the sign small—it was unlikely to have held their attention if they weren't looking for something to distract them from America's grandeur. The tut-tutting over America's small-minded practicality is really a grunt accompanying the effort to keep America within bounds. In a letter home to his wife from Arizona, Ilf revealed the strength of purpose this perspective required. "Excuse me that I have suddenly begun to write all the time about the nature, but the canyons, the desert, the mountains— all this is unusually beautiful, and not to think about it is impossible." In general, however, he and Petrov managed to suppress the urge to describe America's marvels.

Instead, they provided a very detailed picture of surfaces. Though this real America is not totally appealing—Ilf and Petrov assure their readers they would never live here—it is comfortable, almost cozy. It is an America cut down to size. Ilf and Petrov chose their title advisedly. (When their American publisher, hoping to trade on the popularity of their earlier *The Golden Calf,* changed the name of the translated edition to *Little Golden America,* they protested vehemently.) Ideally, America should be seen as a contiguous stretch of small villages, all unsurprising and knowable in all their details. Everything that is too awesome—natural or man-made—is edited out. The jacket illustration on the original edition figures just such a landscape: an S-shaped road with a cluster of unprepossessing buildings (a café with an awning, a tourist camp with a "rest rooms" sign in front) at every curve. The interval between the clusters is minimal and almost totally occupied by billboards, leaving virtually no space for nature to assert itself—a few scraggly trees represent all America has to offer. There is not even a sky. This is an unspectacular and unaggressive America, the true America behind the awesome facade.

There was not, until fairly recently, much visual information for Soviet citizens to use as a check against the written reports. The few Soviet movies about America tended to picture smoke-filled rooms of conspirators from the military-industrial complex, not broad vistas, and anyway they were not filmed on location. American-made movies were difficult, if not impossible, to find. Very few Soviet painters visited America. Television was no more than talking heads. Most Soviet photographers focused on shots of urban injustice; it was hard to get a sense of the American landscape from them.

In the last few years, Russians' idea of what America looks like has changed. Television is responsible. Programs featuring a commentator in a studio sitting in front of a few stills are passé. The changes in the way television went about its business at first seemed purely a matter of technology, a willingness to introduce mechanical innovations; but the changes in technology turned out to have broad cultural consequences. With more on-the-spot reporting, it has become much harder to maintain that every American monument is a false facade, that every one of its marvels can be interpreted away. Point a camera at New York or Washington or Los

Angeles long enough, and you are also going to pick up some proofs of a compelling grandeur.

Signs of strain in the old perspective on America began to be felt somewhere in the mid-1970s. *Contradictory America (Protivore-chivaya Amerika)*, a 1974 television documentary, nicely exemplifies the moment of transition—a sensibility still dedicated to unmasking America's grandeur (the title of the report is telling), yet deflected from this goal by its own methods. The shots of Niagara Falls, for example, are predictably brief, and are only an excuse for the commentator to remark that in general this is a country "where trees and grass do not grow. Knowledgeable people raise their automobile windows: there is a heavy stench—the air is polluted by tens of factories—which stings the eyes, tickles the throat. The grass withers, trees die." These observations are more spiteful than anything in *One-Story America,* but *Contradictory America* nevertheless proves to have the more accommodating vision. When Ilf and Petrov summed up Niagara Falls in a nonchalant sentence, their Soviet readers had no grounds to dispute their judgment; but a picture of Niagara Falls, however brief and even when followed by dismissive commentary, has an enduring force.

As the technology continued to improve, the image of America became still more difficult to control. In *The Man from Fifth Avenue,* a 1983 documentary that was very widely viewed, a Soviet television crew followed an unemployed American on his wanderings through New York City. Rapid montage, hand-held camera, quick close-ups, the whole paraphernalia of modern television reporting was brought to bear. The narration hewed to the old line that public America was mostly a false front, but the images on the screen subverted the words. Each time a shot of an elegant Broadway theater was used as a lead-in to a segment on porno movie houses or there was some jazzy editing meant to prove all our highways were overcrowded, America's allure acquired another increment of credibility. Television refuses to hold still for the strategies of diminishment that Ilf and Petrov concocted.

Gorbachev's *glasnost* has taken the process a step further. The perspective on America's landscape has become much broader, more generous, and it is usually offered up without the nasty accompanying remarks that used to be de rigueur. My stay in Moscow coincided with the publication of a book of photographs called *America: A Heart to Heart Conversation,* with dust jacket blurbs (from Evgeny Evetushenko among others) attesting to its breakthrough status. It is certainly an advance beyond what was possible a couple of years ago. Beginning with the book's cover, which shows the Stars and Stripes majestically unfurled against a backdrop of the New York skyline, there is an easy acceptance of America's grandeur. Our most spectacular sights, including Niagara Falls, the Mississippi, the San Francisco skyline, are shot from angles that confirm their glory. There are also, to be sure, photographs of dreary small towns and urban slums. But—and this is the innovation—there is no suggestion either in the photographs or in the accompanying text that America's problems and trivialities are more true than its power. The landscape is allowed to stand in the fullness of its complicated elements. Perhaps the most striking picture is of Central Park: in the foreground a young man is kicking a football, while young lovers embrace and, slightly off to the side, a group picnics on a large rock; in the background is the full sweep of the Central Park South skyline. America's daily life and its splendors fit within a single frame, a configuration that constitutes a rejection of the earlier Russian travelers' perspective. It follows that even the usually sacrosanct Ilf and Petrov come in for criticism, for failing to give full credit to New York's skyscrapers, "these giants, penetrating the sky." Give America credit, the text and the photographs as much as announce, let it have its full scope.

*America: A Heart to Heart Conversation* shows the achievement of *glasnost*—and also its limits. Though the new perspective on America is closer to the truth (or at least closer to how Americans picture it), it is still just a pretty picture. Looking at images, even full-bodied, head-on images, is not the same as seeing a place. An excellent book of photographs does not alter the fact that most visa applications are still routinely rejected or, if approved, subject to so many restrictions as to make the trip impossible anyway. As it happens, the book's afterword admits its own secondhand quality. "We need today not only to hear and read about America and Americans. We also need to see—in television presentations, documentary films, these kinds of photographs [as are in the book in hand]," it is said, but this self-congratulation fades into a depressing afterthought. "And best of all—to see directly, with one's own eyes, on trips." Russians have come closer to seeing America, but it is still at a crucial remove. Like the people in Plato's Myth of the Cave, Russians see not reality but only reality's shadows (or, perhaps, their contemporary equivalent, electrons playing on a television cathode tube). The difference is that Russians know they are looking at shadows. They yearn for the ultimate reality.

My friend from *SShA* told me, "I sometimes wonder what does an American car driving down an American street look like." The phrase implied a scene filled with the minutiae of daily life, the quick flash of detail that you can see properly only with your own eyes.

A Soviet acquaintance asked me where I lived.

"New Jersey," I answered, naming the town.

"Near New York," she responded proudly. "I have a map at home."

"About an hour away, if the trains run on time," I said.

"Which of course they never do," she said. "Or only by accident."

Taken aback by her perfect mimicking of American suburbanite palaver, I picked up the same intonation. "It's a good place for children," I said. "Nice places to play. Some green grass."

"And when you are not on vacation—what city do you live in then?"

We had, it turned out, only seemed to have been on the same wavelength.

It wasn't the first time that I found such a conversation slipping off into misunderstanding. Russians have a lot of opinions about how we behave, but they have difficulty visualizing the setting of our actions. America presents itself as a conglomeration of values rather than a place. Its appearance—the sheer look of it—has not been grasped. Sometimes I think that Russians go wrong because they try to see America as they see their own country; that perspective is too idiosyncratic to travel very well.

One evening I took a taxi to the neighborhood near the Kursky station, out behind the Kremlin, to visit a man who was a passionate lover of American jazz. We sat in a room stacked with Jazztone records, with sophisticated stereo equipment crowding every corner and bookshelves piled with copies of *Downbeat*. I listened as he talked about his favorite performers, and about the history of American jazz in Russia. "Do you know," he said, "that in the very first May Day parade, on Red Square in 1922, there was a float carrying a jazz band? They played 'Me and My Girl.' " He laughed with pure delight, his head thrown back, and I did too, feeling at that moment the little thrill of sensibilities unexpectedly joining. We lived in different countries, but had enough in common to see irony in the same situation.

We talked until it was almost one o'clock. Public transport slams shut at that hour, and we were in an area where there were sure to be no cruising taxis—getting here, it had taken three packs of Marlboros to convince a cabby to go so far off the beaten track. At the door, buttoning my coat hurriedly, I asked the jazz lover the way to the nearest metro station. "Follow the path water would take," he said.

I walked out into the unlit courtyard, shuffling a bit, hoping my feet would feel any incline my eyes missed. Around the first corner, the street widened into a boulevard that ran perceptibly downhill, and I let momentum carry me. There was no one about and the only traffic was a trolley bus that vanished around a corner, but the silent gloom hardly affected my confidence. I was gliding. Then, two blocks farther on, the boulevard forked. The left fork was broader and better lit, but flat; the right fork was a shadowy, crabbed alley that seemed to decline slightly. I hesitated, then plunged off to the right. The alley curved till it seemed to be describing a circle, darkening as it went. I began to feel apprehensive, partly because of the gloom but even more because I was no longer certain I was going in the right direction. I had not expected such fine judgments would be necessary. Finally I came out onto a new boulevard. I was now in a part of town that in daylight would have been alive with activity but at this hour was empty and bleak, with not one lighted window in any of the houses. I kept moving, trotting faster, propelled by nervous excitement. By the time I saw the red "M" of the Nagibin metro stop, I was running pretty hard and was sweating from the exertion. I made the last train with a few minutes to spare, but I felt more angry than elated. I cursed my jazz-loving friend. His electronic toys and funny anecdotes had taken me in, made me think we understood each other, and I had let his directions pass unquestioned—but really are those the words with which to send someone out into the unfamiliar night?

"Follow the path that water would take." It was only after I had been in Moscow a bit longer that I began to appreciate his perspective. To a foreigner, backstreet Moscow is a hopeless maze, all blind alleys and dead ends. Half the byways don't appear on any map. Crumbling churches spill over onto the sidewalks and the endless sewer repairs cause streets to terminate in impassable rubble. The critic Walter Benjamin noted that "in Moscow the country plays hide-and-seek with the city" and it is so—the demands of the cumbersome earth appear to defeat all regularity. But the natives have come to terms with Moscow in their own fashion. They have a sense of the roll of the landscape, the declensions of the property.

They have grasped the image of the city as whole, as someone might unconsciously memorize the rippling effects of a stone dropped in a smooth pond. At the center is the Kremlin, the first edifice built in what would become Moscow, with its large adjoining square that once served as a marketplace for tradesmen and peasants and as a site of public executions for unfortunates of every class. Around this center is a concentric network of traffic loops, built on the foundations of the fortified ramparts that marked the successive spasms of Moscow's outward growth. Muscovites are often baffled by requests for an address around the next corner; the local chaos defeats them. But every Muscovite can instantly provide minute directions for getting from the most outlying district to the city center. It's as if their comprehension was powered by centrifugal force.

This centrifugal force also exerts a power beyond the city limits, and has social as well as geographical implications. Russians who live outside the capital have always had their attention inordinately drawn to it—it is not only the seat of power, but a living symbol of the whole country, not only itself but an encapsulation of all of Russia. In the tsarist period, what happened in St. Petersburg, especially on the city's central thoroughfare Nevsky Prospect, was taken as an accurate reflection of the state of the nation. Gogol spoke to a comprehending readership when he wrote, "No directory or information bureau will supply such correct information as Nevsky Prospect." When the Bolsheviks moved the seat of government to Moscow, closer to the country's geographical center, it intensified the belief that Russia's capital was like a magnet, drawing to itself the disparate spirit of the most outlying regions. Can people who live in such a country understand America, the look of it, the feel of its structure?

Traveling in an airplane over Washington, D.C., as he reached the end of a trip through the United States in 1957, the Soviet novelist Valentin Kataev looked out the window and remarked, "It was odd and depressing. Wherever I went in the United States, I heard the same thing: This isn't the real America. You have come to the wrong place. Look for the real America anywhere else, but not here. Just keep looking." The old cliché that America is endlessly varied, with no spot that can be called typical, exasperates Russians. Even those who speak knowingly about the details of our culture—whether to blame or to praise—often announce the limits of their comprehension: America as a whole eludes them, they say. After visiting America, the poet Sergei Esenin remarked, "In the specifically American milieu there is a total absence of any real presence," and his comment reflects the anxiety experienced by many of his countrymen. Bemused by memories of Moscow, lodestar of the nation's attention, they find it incomprehensible that there should not be an American counterpart. Assiduously, they continue to track a phantom.

New York City has always been the cynosure of Russian attention, and has been proportionately the object of most complaint. There is too much noise, too much dirt, too much traffic. But the most recurrent objection is not so precise; the dissatisfaction is less with what exists than with what does not. The real New York fails to correspond to the ideal one that Russians have created and that is nurtured by the Russian media. Visiting the city in 1970, Vasily Aksyonov remarked, "You have read so much about the 'streets' and avenues of Manhattan, seen so many photos, films and television, that in your imagination this city is, it can be said, built. You have sketched in everything in your imagination and absolutely know how these streets run, from where to where; but finding yourself in real New York, you suddenly see that you are mistaken, that the streets run not 'from here to there' but 'from there to here.' "

Beginning in the 1920s, when Soviets first began coming as visitors and continuing till this day, the tone of their reports has always had this element of bafflement—what they have encountered is not what they expected. As the acknowledged first city of the country, New York should be the hub from which the rest of America radiates, the comprehensible point which explains the whole; but the reality is otherwise. It proves impossible to grasp the city, to comprehend its meaning. It is too uncentered, altogether too wobbly a thing. "No," Mayakovsky said, adding his stentorian voice to the debate, "New York is not a contemporary city, New York is not organized. Having cars, subways, skyscrapers and such things is not proof of a real industrial culture. [New York] is a gigantic accumulation of objects, created by children, and not a perfected result of the labor of a mature people who understand their desires and work according to a plan, like artists."

Significantly, the rectilinear pattern of Manhattan's streets, which helps to orient most tourists, only irritates Russians; the regularity forms an uncongenial equivalence, lacking some necessary pivot point. Aksyonov's reference to streets that are so much the same that they can be adequately described as running "not from here to there but from there to here" stands in a tradition of exasperated Russian reactions to Manhattan's grid system. According to Ilf and Petrov, who visited in 1931, ". . . the streets are quite indistinguishable and even old New Yorkers cannot tell one street from another by any outward signs," but it is clear that the confusion they attribute to the natives attacked them also. Their tone, usually jaunty, edges toward anxiety. New York is a city, Ilf and Petrov complain, that makes movement a blind tropism; success or failure in reaching one's destination is a matter of luck. ". . . The main shoals of pedestrians and automobiles advance along the wide avenues . . . [while] hordes of indignant unfortunates and maniacs gather in the dirty narrow lanes to traverse the city crosswise, not lengthwise."

If not in New York, perhaps the essence of America can be discovered elsewhere. Over the years other candidates have been put forward. For a while Chicago served, its stockyards providing perfect symbols for the workings of the American system in general; "The Factory of Death," Vladimir Korolenko called it in one of his stories, and he had in mind not only the slaughterhouses, nor the city in which these were located, but all of America, where cruelty for profit was the rule. In the 1970s, *Izvestia*'s long-time American correspondent, Boris Kondrashev, staked a claim for California. He announced that his book, *Appointment with California,* was "an experiment to discover America through its most populous and, if you please, most dynamic state, where there can be seen, clearly and sharply, as in a magnifying glass, the features of contemporary American society." Other Russians have nominated Texas or Washington, D.C.; Detroit also has occasionally been invested with the element of typicality, its curve from boom to bust prefiguring capitalism's demise. It's not an outrageous method, to claim the part for the whole, but in Russians it reaches a fanatical degree. They must have the still point in a turning world, their center which explains the periphery. Otherwise they are at a loss.

Since the larger design of America baffles them, Russians tend to focus instead on the details, hoping that these will serve as reference points on which to hinge their imagination. They inventory our topographical features with the passionate finickiness of a dedicated accountant. Indeed, aspects of America that other nations have long since accepted as utterly familiar still preoccupy Russians. The abutting slums and mansions, the highly trafficked highways, the sweeping bridges—Russians still find this worthy of excited comment. Most of all, however, it is the skyscraper that claims their attention. The urban skyline is to them no mere cliché of modernity but rather remains an urgent issue, evoking positions ranging from admiration to ridicule. At the hotel newsstand, I picked up the weekly newspaper *Nedelya* and read a report on his trip to America by Mikhail Zhvanetsky, a popular satirist. "The most beautiful thing in America is the skyscraper. Skyscrapers, as someone once said, are terribly sexual. America protrudes into the air. Cities protrude upward, firm and far. Run your palm along the edge of [this vista] of skyscrapers—and you'll cut yourself. The center of the cities protrudes, the different neighborhoods protrude, Manhattan protrudes, Chicago protrudes, Boston protrudes." It would be hard to imagine any other country for whom the American skyscraper is the occasion of such jejune naughtiness; but, of course, such language is also its own sort of compliment, an admission that skyscrapers present a vista too powerful to be described by common speech.

Skyscrapers disturb Russians for good reason. They seem as much ideological concepts as they are architecture, and as such they have important native implications. Soviet Russia is a country that has always defined itself in terms of modernity. The Revolution was not only a political but a cultural event, meant to create a society fit for the twentieth century. The key Marxist notion of man bending nature to his spirit was wholeheartedly endorsed, and Soviet Russia threw itself headlong into the industrial age singing the praises of the machine and technology. To such a country, skyscrapers are not just a pile of rocks. They are the epitome of modern times.

Soviet poets have almost certainly been more rapturous on the subject of the skyscraper than poets of any other nation, including America. "A dynamo," a structure that "threw a gauntlet in the face of gravity," Mayakovsky called it. These phrases, and a thousand similar ones, were not merely metaphors spun out of the imagination; they were attempts at realistically describing the imminent future. The skyscraper was a key part of the world that seemed on the verge of being born right down the street. The Bolsheviks put urban planning high on their agenda, intending to transform the cities of the Soviet society into places where the citizens could be efficiently organized into "mass action," and the skyscraper was often a key element of these schemes. As Alexander Blok put it in a poem entitled "New America," "I see huge factories of many stories / And workers' cities clustering round."

It was largely due to the ironies of history, those unexpected linkages of events and meanings, that this initial enthusiasm gave way to ambivalence. Though the regime wanted to make the skyscraper an essential part of the New Society, it had to confront the fact that the skyscraper already existed elsewhere. As such, it could well be damaged goods, ideologically speaking. To the Russians, architecture was politics, and the skyscraper's habitation in nations politically at odds with socialism could not be dismissed as happenstance.

More precisely, Russians had to confront the fact that America (as the title of Blok's poem conceded) was undeniably the home of the skyscraper, so much so that many Russians believed it defined the very essence of Amerikanizm. Alexander Pasternak, the founder of the Association of Contemporary Architects, noted, "[The sky-scraper] corresponds exactly to the American character, for which any waste of time is anathema." Russian representations of the skyscraper seemed hardly able to resist America's tacit claims to priority. What was perhaps the most ambitious skyscraper design in the Soviet Union, El Lissitzky's "Cloud Project," was an explicit homage to the set-back towers made famous by New York City in the 1920s. Kazimir Malevich entitled his collage "Suprematist Building Among American Skyscrapers," and incorporated photographs of the New York skyline into the work. Even in the august halls of the architectural establishment, America's influence was granted: the winner of the highly publicized competition to build a Palace of Soviets borrowed many of his principles from the design of the Empire State Building, which had deeply impressed him during a visit in 1935.

More precisely, the proposed Palace of Soviets was scaled to be slightly taller than the Empire State Building it was modeled on—a neat practical application of the Marxist principle that communism would reach its apogee not by ignoring capitalism's achievements but by subsuming them. Increasingly, the debate required a sharp competitive edge. Mayakovsky, who loved the skyscraper in principle, insisted that the American version was a grotesque distortion, ". . . comparable to putting ribbons on a steam engine. This is not the art of the industrial century." Given the all too obvious fact that Russia's own skyscrapers were not yet erected, this comment suggests the bravado of a boxer who proclaims victory before stepping into the ring. But Mayakovsky's words also have the late-comer's desperation, common to Russians of that period. The Soviet Union would not cede priority to others, it would blaze its own path—but too often it seemed that some other country (very often America) had gotten there first.

On his way to Hollywood, the film director Sergei Eisenstein stopped briefly in New York, giving him a chance to survey the fabled structures at firsthand: "As your 90-horsepower motor pulls you jerkily from block to block along the steep-cliffed streets, your eyes wander over the smooth surfaces of the skyscrapers. Notions lazily crawl through your brain: 'Why don't they seem high?' 'Why should they, with all their height, still seem cozy, domestic, small town?' . . . You suddenly realize what 'trick' the skyscrapers play on you: although they have many floors, each floor is quite low. Seen directly, the soaring skyscraper appears to be built of a number of small-town buildings, piled on top of each other. One merely needs to go beyond the city limits, or in a few cities merely beyond the center of the city, in order to see the same buildings piled up on top of each other not by the dozens, or fifties, or hundreds, but laid out in endless rows of one- and two-storied stores and cottages along Main Street, or along half-rural side streets." Eisenstein's remarkable attempt to miniaturize New York symbolized the Soviet predicament. American achievements seemed so imposing that only by a leap of the imagination could a Russian try to come to terms with them; but the unintended comedy of Eisenstein's effort also shows that America could not simply be wished away.

Not surprisingly, given its tendencies to reduce life to bureaucratic measures, the regime's ultimate solution to the problem of American influence was an administrative one. A 1947 decree, signed by Stalin, explicitly forbade any copying of foreign styles in the design of Soviet buildings. This drove Russian interest in American architecture into a corner, but it did not kill it. Indeed, it's worth emphasizing that the current fascination with American skyscrapers (the article in *Nedelya* that I saw was only the tip of an iceberg) is a link in an unbroken tradition, not an abrupt eruption made possible by *glasnost*. The American skyscraper is part of the Russian understanding of modern society, an aspect of their utopian dreams, a means to conceptualize technological possibilities; but in truth the best place to look for proof of its persisting allure is not in the Russian imagination but in the Moscow skyline. Some of the signature features of the American skyscraper, supposedly relegated by Stalin's decree to some dustbin of architectural history, can be spied out against these low-lying northern skies, a sort of bricks-and-mortar return of the repressed. The most compelling examples are the seven huge buildings ringing the city center. Decorated with sumptuous iconography celebrating communism, they seem at first glance to be testimony to the doctrine of Socialist Realism; but, paradoxically, they also carry strong traces of the ideas of American architects Harvey Wiley Corbett and Hugh Ferriss, strong proponents of the wedding-cake-style buildings and skyscraper zones that helped create modern New York City. The agent of this cross-cultural pollination was one Vyacheslav Oltarzhevsky, who worked in New York City architectural firms in the 1920s and then returned to an influential post in Moscow. But the ground had been prepared by the complex power, part attraction, part repulsion, that the topography of America exerts over almost all Russians.

On Leningrad's Nevsky Prospect there is a six-story gray cement structure that houses one of the Soviet Union's largest bookstores. It is called Dom Knigi (House of Books). But when it was built in 1907, this was the Russian headquarters of the Singer Sewing Machine Company of Chicago. The Singer company had decided that Russia was on the verge of a bourgeois era and that sewing machines would soon be in great demand; to help make its name well known to potential customers, Singer planned a building with an imposing tower. Originally it was to be eleven stories high, but a city ordinance set an upper limit no higher than the tsar's palace. Making do, Singer instead added other features, though with dubious results. A Soviet guidebook describes the building as "adorned with a pretentious decor in bad taste, which includes a tower topped with a glass sphere, the whole thing completely out of harmony with the somber lines of the Nevsky Prospect. In the evening a light would appear inside the glass sphere, and the name of the firm would sparkle round a metal ring."

A Russian acquaintance, very knowing about things American, once told me jokingly that it was to atone for this instance of colossally bad American taste that the famous dancer Isadora Duncan threw over her long-time lover, Paris Singer, heir to the family fortune, and took up instead with the Soviet poet Sergei Esenin. I laughed, though I was a bit discomfited. It was flattering to find a Russian who knew enough about American social history to make such complicated jokes, but the easy condescension annoyed me. I didn't have the presence of mind to make the retort I should have—that the globe on the building's summit, which once proclaimed the Singer company name, is now ablaze advertising the current occupant, Dom Knigi. For all their disdain of American architecture, Russians still make use of it.

## five

# Cultural
# Exchange

❖

Americandancers, musicians, rock stars, comics (circus and stand-up varieties), performance artists, what have you—march in bat-talions across Russia under the banner of cultural exchange. Of course it's been going on for a long time, this deployment of Amer-ican talent for Soviet review. Almost as soon as the Revolution established itself, American writers and musicians and painters (men like Mark Van Doren, Leopold Stokowski, Lincoln Steffens) formed the American Agency for Cultural Ties with the Soviet Union; and artists continued to tour Russia even during the worst of the Cold War. But with the new hospitality of the Gorbachev regime, the traffic has risen to unprecedented, almost rush-hour levels. There may soon be a gridlock of the journeying artists near, say, Luxembourg. The movement of talent in the name of inter-national friendship has been so spectacular that only the mean-spirited would pause and ask: What is it that these cultural exchanges actually exchange?

While I was in Moscow, the musical review *Sophisticated Ladies,* recently on Broadway, was booked into the Hotel Rossiya's re-splendent theater for two weeks, thence to proceed on tour to Leningrad and Tbilisi. On my way over to have a look at one of the rehearsals, I glanced through the program which had been given to me. It spoke of historical breakthroughs, summoning up an image of cultures heaving into a new spiritual alignment. But grand joinings are often stymied by the jaggedness of their details, and upon arriving at the theater I saw how easily things could slip out of kilter. The marquee was in English; when I asked why, I was told that it was to have been in Russian until someone realized that a literal rendering—*Prekrasnye ledis*—could be construed to mean prostitutes.

That was only one of a series of crossed cultural connections. Members of the company with whom I had a chance to talk had complaints ranging from unpalatable food to the natives' insistence on speaking Russian. The Cyrillic alphabet made the street signs gibberish, and members of the troupe got lost almost as soon as they exited the hotel. It wasn't much better within the hotel, a structure so huge it was like a small country; getting from point to point required a careful itinerary, and the surly hotel staff, instead of helping, behaved like border guards. Most important, the rehearsals were not going well. The company's director told me that the local stagehands were driving her crazy. The elaborate sets—one consisted of several hundred flashing lights in the form of a seductively supine woman and spanned the width of the stage—demanded technological agility, and the Russians tried to mask their ineptitude by debating before every movement. "I'll take Broadway, even with all the union nonsense you have to put up with," the director announced wearily. "How will this show ever come together? I'm counting on a miracle."

I was curious to see what would come out of this buzz of confusion and complaint, and got tickets by pulling some strings. (A telephone call, mention of my U.S. citizenship, a bottle of vodka—the usual procedure.) The audience on the evening I attended was composed largely of grumpy bureaucrats and their wives; hearing Duke Ellington's music was probably less important to them than showing they had the influence to get hold of a difficult ticket. A smattering of diplomats, correspondents, and tourists was present out of a sense of cultural *noblesse oblige,* Westerners perfunctorily honoring Western products. Very distinct from the rest of the audience was a group of twenty or so Russians, seated together near the back of the auditorium, who were talking and gesticulating excitedly. They turned out to be of a legendary breed—those Russian jazz fans who throughout the bleak pre-*glasnost* years had spent long nights tuning their shortwave radios to Willis Conover's famous program on Voice of America "Music USA." Seeing and hearing this same music performed in the Hotel Rossiya by an American orchestra must have been as dizzying as having one's illicit fantasy suddenly acclaimed as a great creative achievement.

It was, all in all, an audience of strong preconceptions, already disposed to ennui or excitement. What was lacking, I decided, was a fair representation of the average Soviet citizen who might have looked at this bit of Americana with an innocent eye. As far as I could tell there was only one couple in the hall who met this standard; I knew because they were there through my good offices. Approaching the theater, I had been stopped by a man who asked if I had any tickets for sale. From his forlorn look it was clear he hadn't much hope. When I produced two extras and asked for no more than the official price, he almost laughed out loud at his good luck. He insisted that I accept a couple of rubles extra—he felt more comfortable with a traditional scalping transaction than with some inexplicable miracle.

Made loquacious by the happy turn of events, the man struck up a conversation as soon as we settled into our adjoining seats. He was in Moscow for a short visit, he told me, just for a few days of fun. "I come to Moscow rarely, when the pressure can no longer be resisted." He cocked an eyebrow in the direction of his wife, a stout, stolid woman who was staring at the lowered curtain as if trying to decipher a meaning in its folds. "She likes Moscow. I would as soon stay in Pyatigorsk."

The mention of that remote town in the Caucasus piqued my interest. Pyatigorsk is the setting of the great nineteenth-century novel *A Hero of Our Time,* and it was marvelous to meet a living and breathing inhabitant. Indeed, the more my neighbor talked, the more I decided he could have stepped from the pages of Lermontov's novel. The character Maksim Maksimych has become synonymous in Russia with bluff good nature, with friendliness to strangers; my neighbor was a perfect copy of Maksim Maksimych, though—sign of the times—he was the head of a biogenetic lab and not a retired army sergeant like the original. "The mountains around Pyatigorsk are wonderful, like magic," he told me, perfectly echoing the words and spirit of the novel. "Hunting, climbing, fishing—who needs Moscow?" He gave a sidelong glance at his wife, whose pose had not changed but who nonetheless seemed to express disapproval of his chatting with a foreigner. He shrugged, doing a little imitation of guilt for my benefit. We were males bonding together, which was also Maksim Maksimych's favorite mode of behavior.

The curtain parted to reveal the huge silhouette of the reclining woman, all lights properly lit and all pieces in place as far as I could tell, and the dancers and singers began working their way through the Ellington corpus. The audience reacted much as I would have expected. The Russian bureaucrats and their wives took it in coolly and blandly, much as if they were listening to a report on kolkhoz production capacity. The foreign diplomats nodded in cool approval at this proof of American cultural dexterity. And the claque of jazz-lovers burst into thunderous applause as soon as the orchestra played the few notes they needed to identify the melody, and they stamped their feet and whistled at the song's conclusion.

I preferred to watch my neighbor's reaction. At least it was unpredictable. His attention occasionally wandered, and sometimes he seemed more interested in the design of the ceiling or even the contours of the armrest than in what was happening onstage. His comments on the performance were sudden and delphic. When a black woman with a thin, sweet voice started in on "Caravan," a song often played on Voice of America, the jazz-lover's section vibrated and hummed like an airplane gearing up for take-off. Noticing this, my neighbor declared, "The audience believes this singer requires special encouragement." When the orchestra swung into "Take the A Train" and the set was rearranged to depict 125th Street, he whispered meaningfully, "Harlem will always be Harlem." A dancer's strut to the beat of "It Don't Mean a Thing" prompted the observation, "She's a mulatto, I think." A few minutes later there was a qualification. "Of course her skin is very light." And then, finally, he offered an emphatic conclusion, as if he had at last worked through all the data. "But her hair is definitely a Negro's, you have to agree."

I wasn't prepared to get into an ethnographic argument, and so I only nodded in a way meant to suggest his observations had been duly noted. The truth was I had no idea what he was talking about. We might as well have been watching different performances. I asked myself: Was this, then, what is meant by cultural exchange? To judge from my neighbor, the transaction was more than a bit erratic.

The final curtain came down and the audience began to disperse. I caught the sleeve of my Maksim Maksimych just as his wife started tugging him off to the aisle. I wanted to ask him one question. I knew I could trust the honesty of his response.

"What was the single most impressive element of what you saw tonight?" I asked him.

"The technology," he said without hesitating. "The lighting, the way the sets were moved around and all that. I didn't think our boys could do all that stuff, but I guess we showed you *Shtatniki.*"

His comment was not, as it happened, precisely correct (he underestimated how much the Americans had helped with the staging), but the drift was worth attending to. In marking off the Russian contribution, my Maksim Maksimych had made clear that whatever cultural exchange may be, it is not an occasion to be any more grateful than was absolutely required.

American artists arrive in the U.S.S.R. virtually aglow with an appreciation of their own generosity—they are certain they are providing culture to the deprived. Russians find this assessment ridiculous. They are fiercely proud of their artistic traditions, and confident that the rest of the world values them also. That anyone would condescend to Russia culturally astounds the natives. That Americans would do so, also exasperates them. The image of an America bestowing cultural favors has been rendered morally dubious by historical events.

One particularly lurid example is the story of the 1904 St. Louis World's Fair. Russian artists consigned six hundred of their paintings to be put on exhibit. Several of the works were of high artistic value, including some by Repin, Vereshchagin, and Roerich (who was later to design the sets for Stravinsky's *Rite of Spring*), but none attracted a buyer. A Russian merchant acting as the artists' agent thereupon shipped the paintings to New York with the intention of putting them up for auction, but at that point U.S. customs officials intervened and impounded all but one or two in lieu of unpaid tariffs. There followed eight years of litigation, chicanery, and double-dealing. The artists themselves, who had a financial as well as artistic stake in the fate of their works, were ignored. It became mostly an American affair, with a California financier contesting a New York lawyer for control of the paintings sitting in a government warehouse. When an auction was finally held in 1912—some paintings going for two or three dollars—the government collected the amount due on the unpaid tariffs. The Russian agent and the artists got nothing. And the paintings passed conclusively into American hands. Some were eventually bought by museums and others vanished into private collections. Danilov-Uralsky's *Forest Fire* ended up, after complicated peregrinations through American society, in the Visiting Room of the Anheuser-Busch Brewery in St. Louis—a particularly neat example of how these pieces of Russian culture were fully absorbed into the American way of life. How much gratitude, on such a balance sheet, is due a road company's performance of *Sophisticated Ladies*?

In fact, our appropriation of Russian culture has rarely been as blatant as in the case of the St. Louis Fair paintings, but the result has been much the same. America accumulated what Russia lost.

The tides of history have flowed to our advantage, and our Yankee trader tradition has also helped. The coming of the Revolution, for example, which to Russians signified the end of feudalism and the beginning of socialism, Lenin instead of the Romanovs, and a whole array of other momentous changes—to American collectors meant that there were bargains to be had. When Russian aristocrats rushed to sell treasured heirlooms, either to get much-needed cash or to forestall appropriation by the Bolsheviks, Americans were on the spot to take advantage. William Boyce Thompson, a copper magnate who was the head of the Red Cross mission in Petrograd in 1917 remarked in a letter home, "I cannot help feeling sorry for a lot of the titled families, as a lot of them have sold out, and I think most of them will sell their valuable works of art or their homes." Feelings of sympathy did not deter him long, however. A few days later he wrote to his wife, "I am sending a [railroad] carload of [antique] furniture and objects." He needed this vehicle and more. In the space of a year or so he managed to acquire porcelain vases, old masters such as Fragonard, and large portions of the furniture belonging to the Crown Prince. Americans were so shrewd in getting in on a good thing that the knock-down auctions where valuable items went for a song were referred to as "American auctions."

Thanks to the aristocracy's selling spree, the Bolsheviks assumed control of a nation that had lost much that was valuable both financially and culturally. At first some of the new leaders hardly minded the cultural depletion. Since they intended to create a pure proletarian culture, they saw nothing to regret in the loss of some exemplars of the outmoded bourgeois aesthetic. In that heady springtime of communism, the commissars insisted that a painting of a red-cheeked woman astride a tractor was worth three of Venus rising demurely from the sea. But as common sense replaced euphoria, the attitude toward prerevolutionary Russia changed. The old aristocracy's paintings and jewelry and fine furniture were pronounced suitable for workers to enjoy, part of the heritage they had acquired. With this realization came the correlative one that foreigners—Americans, preeminently—who had removed items of cultural significance were not much better than buccaneers.

This judgment was not much altered when the regime subsequently decided itself to sell off some of the art treasures that had come into its possession. The Soviets sold voluntarily, in the sense that no one was pointing a gun at their head; but their hand was forced by a need for hard currency. There was no reason to look kindly on those who took advantage of their economic hardship. In 1929, Commissar of Trade Anastas Mikoyan told the American entrepreneur Armand Hammer, "You can have the pictures, that's all right. . . . But we will make a revolution and take them back." The words ring with desperate bravado; no revolution was imminent. In those desperate times, large chunks of Russia's cultural heritage had to be yielded. To the Library of Congress went the library of Nicolas II—50,000 volumes at less than a dollar a book. From the Hermitage in Leningrad, Andrew Mellon acquired Titian's *Venus with Mirror,* Rembrandt's *Joseph Accused by Potiphar's Wife,* and Raphael's *Alba Madonna.* Ambassador Joseph E. Davies and his wife, Marjorie Merriweather Post, stocked up on valuable porcelains which they shipped back to Hillwood, their Washington, D.C., estate. The government's policy largely accomplished its economic purpose—the sales to Mellon alone brought in $7 million, which was almost one-third of the amount earned by all other exports to America in 1930—but there was little recompense for the harm done to the nation's sense of identity.

Armand Hammer (who apparently was given special export privileges as a reward for reconstructing the Soviet asbestos industry), performed a particularly vivid exploit of cultural alchemy, taking items that were deep-dyed Russian and transforming them into items that fit seamlessly into American life. The tsarist porcelains and furniture that he obtained he put up for sale in stores like Lord & Taylor, making them available to every New York housewife with some spare change. The marketing was so successful that Hammer redoubled his commercial efforts, stocking La Vieille Russie wholly with treasures from the tsarist aristocracy.

What must it have been like for a Russian visitor strolling down Fifth Avenue to pass this store and see its glittering window display? I tried to imagine, by way of orientation, passing Moscow's GUM department store and seeing Washington's watch or Jefferson's furniture up for sale.

In those interwar years, a huge number of objects—porcelains, paintings, jewelry—were sucked away westward, vanishing forever over the horizon. What once was Russian became American, a perfectly common physical displacement that left deep emotional scars. But objects have not been the most poignant loss. Over the years, beginning right after the Revolution and continuing to the present moment, a large number of Russian artists have departed their homeland. Some left by choice, some at the point of a gun; some were looking for more artistic freedom, some for more money. The motives were mixed, the results ambiguous, but one constant has been the destination. America has been the favored haven of so many of the émigré artists that a Russian looking at our culture from a particular angle might believe he was looking at a refraction of his own tradition. Artists, it is said, are citizens of the world, bound to no one place; listening to their music, watching them dance, one sees aspects of the eternal. But in practice this doesn't wash. Jascha Heifetz was a great violinist, but listening to his music, no Russian will fail to note that he was a great violinist who was trained in Odessa and lived out his days in California. It's not a question of technique, but of a pervasive aura.

The list of eminent émigré artists is long, spanning many fields— Horowitz, Nabokov, Vishniak, and more recently Baryshnikov, Makarova, Rostropovich, Solzhenitsyn, among many others. But in some ways the loss of less famous artists has been more galling. The gritty fabric of American culture, the material that forms a constant backdrop for more spectacular creative flights, often seems to bear a label saying "made in Russia." Would *Destry Rides Again* have been the same minus Mischa Auer's comic accent? How much would have been lost if Tennessee Williams' plays had been staged without Boris Aronson's sets? Would American musical taste have evolved as fast if the Budapest String Quartet (all of them Russian émigrés) had not toured up and down the country? Russian talent has performed much of the hard labor of American culture, and in the process became thoroughly integrated into the landscape.

For a long time the official strategy for dealing with this unfavorable balance of cultural trade was to adopt a pose of unconcern. Those artists who emigrated were most often simply ignored. When they were mentioned, the tone was condescending—only fools would give up the glories of an artist's life in the fatherland. Russian culture was better off without them. But that strategy has now been largely abandoned. Citizens who had been taught to accommodate the steady diminishment of the nation's culture are now being allowed to ask if it wasn't all a bad mistake. The result is confusion and anger.

The welter of emotions crystallized most memorably during the recent visit of Vladimir Horowitz to Moscow. Horowitz's career reached its apogee in the West, but he already had a reputation before he emigrated from the Soviet Union in 1926. The audience at the performances treated him as a Russian who had merely been on loan to the world. With their numerous curtain calls and bouquets for the artist and Russian exclamations, the Muscovites insisted on his ancestry. If applause sustained long enough and loud enough could have done the trick, Horowitz would have walked out of the recital hall with a Soviet passport, and a missing treasure would have been restored to the nation.

While strolling along Gorky Street I noticed an advertisement in the lobby of the Ermolaev Theater announcing the next production, and it stopped me dead in my tracks. Alongside the title was a photograph of the author, Vladimir Nabokov. The son of a prominent prerevolutionary liberal, a self-exile from Russia in 1920, he wandered through the cultural backwaters of the emigration in Berlin and Paris before he won fame and fortune in America with the publication of *Lolita*—his career made him the very embodiment of the artist that Russia had lost or, as often, spurned. Though *samizdat* translations of his novels circulated among the intelligentsia, Nabokov was persona non grata with the regime. Official Russia knew of his American reputation, but shrugged him off as a bourgeois aesthete and insisted they couldn't understand what all the fuss was about. Once when I was in Leningrad and in a devotional mood, I took a pilgrimage to the house off St. Isaac's Square, where Nabokov had spent part of his boyhood. Entering, I found myself in some sort of office. The manager came rushing down the stairs to bar my intrusion. "This is a place of work," he informed me with annoyance. "Not a museum." A post office or perhaps a grocery store would have been bad enough, but this was the ultimate kiss-off; nothing was more inimical to Nabokov than the plodding, workaday Soviet bureaucracy.

For his part Nabokov accepted the breach caused by the Revolution with a vengeance. He shucked his Russian skin almost completely and made himself over into an American writer. Not only did he use America as the setting for his novels but—rarest of writing miracles—switched from his native language to English. In his works, Russia figures only as a paradise lost, a land that to all intents and purposes ceased to exist after 1917. Solzhenitsyn, perhaps the only émigré writer comparable in fame and stature, has kept up a bitter dispute with the land he left behind, arguing about everything from religion to resettlement of the northern tundras. When Nabokov left in 1919,he never looked back, preferring the Russia that he carried about in his imagination. Russia would have to change immeasurably before he would have thought of returning.

Seemingly it has, at least enough so that his posthumous return could be announced publicly and with flourishes. The work the Ermolaev was planning to stage, a dramatization of the novel *Invitation to an Execution,* was a particularly provocative choice, since its theme is totalitarianism's attack on the individual imagination. But anything by Nabokov would have been startling.

When I telephoned Valery Fokine, the artistic director of the Ermolaev, and told him that as an undergraduate at Cornell I had listened to Nabokov's lectures, it piqued his interest. He invited me to give a talk to the company about Nabokov's style and habits. Anything that gave the actors a deeper appreciation of the author would enrich their performance, he said. I spent an evening writing out some notes. I had lectured on Nabokov in American universities fairly often, but this was going to be different—explaining the conquering hero to the land that once scorned him is not just a day at the beach.

I found Fokine in his office at the back of the theater. He was in his late thirties, boyish-looking, and with a manner that was simultaneously fretful and distracted, as if he were worried but couldn't remember why. He wore yellow socks and a red sweater under his dark suit jacket—inside many a somber Soviet citizen, it is said, there is a dandy struggling to get out. A television set was on in the corner, broadcasting a soccer match. As we chatted desultorily, Fokine occasionally glanced in that direction. He did not mention Nabokov, and indeed I noticed that the furniture in the room was not set up for a lecture. After a few minutes, Fokine motioned for me to follow him. As we made our way through the backstage clutter, I concentrated on the Nabokovian pun with which I planned to begin my talk.

Fokine led me through the wings and onto the stage. It was bare, except for a few props. There were only two other people present. This also, I realized, was not going to be the site of any lecture. Instead, Fokine suggested that I might enjoy watching the rehearsal.

"It's our first run-through and we have never done anything by Nabokov before. Perhaps you can give us some ideas," he said. I sat down on one of the chairs on the stage while Fokine and two actors began to plot out the opening scene—the hero awakes to find himself in prison, condemned to die for the crime of being opaque in a land where everyone else is transparent.

After an interval, Fokine turned to me. "The audience will be seated on the stage. This will make them see that questions of social conformity, of private imagination, are not just a spectacle with no connection to our own way of life today."

He paused, waiting for a reply. I could think of no direct response to his pronouncement, and instead I said, "You know Nabokov had the English title as *Invitation to a Beheading*. That works better than the Russian, don't you think?"

Fokine considered this information without much enthusiasm. "Ah yes, the focus of imagination severed from the physical self," he said at last. "I suppose the ideal presentation would be to have the actors play their roles carrying their heads in their hands."

He didn't seem to think much of that line of attack, however, and he turned back to the actors and resumed the run-through. The rehearsal went on for an hour, concentrating on the nuts-and-bolts of staging, the plotting of movement, the lighting, that sort of thing, which soon lost its interest for me. For his part, having apparently satisfied the obligation to ask my opinion, Fokine seemed to have totally forgotten my presence. I shuffled through my notes, wondering when my audience would appear.

Finally, Fokine adjourned the rehearsal. "Let's go," he said to me, and we retraced our path back to his office. We didn't pass anyone en route, no one, at least, who looked eager to learn about Nabokov's personal mannerisms. In his office, Fokine once more flipped on the television—the soccer match was still in progress, and he considered it ruefully. Then, unexpectedly, he reached into his desk and produced a bottle of grade-A vodka, a luxury item these days in Moscow. He extended it to me. "Take this as a commemoration of our acquaintance," he said. "Visitors from America are welcome, but especially students of Nabokov."

We had, I realized, somehow gone from pleasant beginning to gracious ending without ever having passed through the substance of the middle. The announced purpose of the occasion, my talk about Nabokov, had not even begun to materialize, and here I was poised on the verge of departure.

Just then, as Fokine and I stood in an awkward stalemate, a

bouncy woman of thirty or so came bustling into the room, then stopped in confusion when she saw me. She apologized for her interruption, but Fokine waved it off. When she continued to look at me inquiringly, he explained who I was and grudgingly, I thought, mentioned my relationship to Nabokov.

"Really?!" she exclaimed. "What was it like, listening to his lectures?"

I chose one of the anecdotes I had prepared. "His wife sat onstage for every one of his lectures, like some sort of *éminence grise*. When he didn't know something he would turn to her for help."

"Ah, but we know all that," Fokine said.

I reached for more Nabokovia. "He read the dictionary. He wrote his novels on three-by-five index cards. He never had a permanent home after leaving Russia, preferring hotels or rented rooms."

"We know that, too," Fokine remarked good-naturedly. "We've done our homework."

They had indeed—they had studied the topic so assiduously that my lecture would have been superfluous. But then why had I been invited in the first place? Could it have been, I wondered, to give flesh to what otherwise would have been only an abstraction: their recouping of a national cultural treasure? I was, along with all his other ex-students, a sort of honorary curator of Nabokov's career. Now that Russians intended to reassume their rightful duties, my services were no longer needed. My enthusiasm for Nabokov had in fact faded a bit since the days I listened to his lectures, but such niceties probably didn't matter to Fokine. I had known and valued Nabokov in his American days, and now I was present in Moscow—the ceremony of investiture could proceed.

Before I left I put one question to Fokine. "To whom would you say Nabokov belongs—to Russia or America?"

"Perhaps he is both of ours now," he answered diplomatically. But I didn't believe for an instant that he truly thought so.

• • •

The emigration of their artists especially dismays Russians because the traffic has been persistently one-way. Many American artists have passed through Russia, and some claimed that the trip was invigorating—Rockwell Kent, Lincoln Steffens, and, more recently, Arthur Miller and John Updike have all had good things to say. Nevertheless, no major American artist has stayed on to practice his craft. The most disturbing case is surely Paul Robeson, since there were many good reasons for him to stay on after he visited Russia in 1934. He admired the people and the politics and had a fair grasp of the language. He was received royally—honored at gala parties, taken on extensive tours, and given special rooms at the Hotel National. Sergei Eisenstein was especially attentive, arranging a special reception at Dom Kino, where Robeson was greeted by a cheering crowd. For his part, Robeson was deeply impressed by Eisenstein's work, and told a reporter that he considered "*The General Line* easily the finest film I've seen." Working together seemed the next natural step. Eisenstein had a script in mind about Toussaint L'Overture and the slave revolution in Haiti, and the two men had passionate discussions on the topic. But nothing came of this or any other project in Russia. The country, Robeson said, had let him feel "like a human being for the first time since I grew up," and he had grown so fond of it that he left his son behind in Moscow to be educated. But he himself departed to continue his career in the West.

Russians can never reconcile themselves to such treatment. They believe, despite the evidence, that their country is a hospitable place for artists. They know all about the nosy bureaucracies, the dreary economy, the unforgiving climate, but they manage to add these up to something less than conclusive condemnation. From the outside, Russia appears to have a sign on the door: "Abandon imagination, all ye who enter," but the inhabitants believe their culture is zipping along just fine, and the long queues for every ballet performance, movie, and poetry reading tend to back them up.

Explaining this phenomenon, Russians shrug their shoulders and refer to intangibles—the Russian soul, the popular spirit, respect for the arts learned at one's mother's knee. How does all this get transmitted to the individual artist? Perhaps it's carried along in the air. Commenting on the part of his boyhood that James Whistler spent in Russia, N. C. Chopadaev, a leading expert on American art, wrote: "The seven years in St. Petersburg, precisely during the years when all the human feelings, thoughts and inclinations were being formulated, could not have passed without a trace in the memory of the artist. In the clear harmonious severity of Whistler's early paintings there is indeed something congenial and close to the transparency and clear beauty of Petersburg." As art criticism, this is a bit fanciful. Whistler left Russia at thirteen, and his brief training in the Imperial Academy was in a style he soon came to scorn. But as an effort to shore up Russia's stature as a haven for the artistic sensibility—in particular, the American artistic sensibility—it is right on the mark.

Russians are a reading people. The bookstores are always crowded, and have been even in periods when literature was dulled by being made to toe the Party line. Moscow subway cars sometimes have the hush of libraries, every passenger engrossed in a book. Russians read a lot of trash, but a surprising number also know their classics. A bus driver once got me to move to the rear by shouting Pushkin at me—he probably had the lines drilled into him as a schoolboy, but it was his adult sense of what was valuable that let him quote them still. Russians consider literature the flagship of the arts, hands down. It has a moral as well as aesthetic purpose, and authors are treated with the respect other countries reserve for religious leaders. With all this, it's nice to see they like American literature.

It's more than curiosity for the unknown; other foreign literatures do not rank as high. For a number of reasons, ranging from the aesthetic to the political and with a lot of the bizarrely idiosyncratic in between, American writers inspire particular allegiance. "We felt an odd intimacy with the American writers of our generation," Vasily Aksyonov has written. "Our destinies were different and our lives developed differently but, when we would meet, we somehow looked into each other's eyes in a particular way, as if we were searching in them for some kind of invisible, common childhood."

Such a remark, which fairly catches the mood before Gorbachev's rise to power, is of course less literary criticism than a lover's mournful cry. American literature has often been tantalizingly just out of reach, familiar yet not fully accessible. Politics has been at fault. The Soviet regime chose to make literature one of the main battlefields of the Cold War—the usual scenario was Americans charging boisterously under the banner of freedom of expression, the Russians clumsily shielding themselves behind claims of anti-Soviet propaganda. Books were banned, book fairs boycotted, authors reviled. Soviet criticism has at one time or another anathematized John Dos Passos, Mary McCarthy, Norman Mailer, Henry Miller, among many others. Though the flow of forbidden books into Soviet territory was never fully blocked—the diplomatic pouch was one unstoppable method—it was sometimes reduced to a mere trickle. At times it was possible to read certain American authors only in *samizdat* editions, which circulated hand to hand.

There is a promise of change in the air. Even those who have doubts about other aspects of *perestroika* are sure that there will be full access to American literature in the near future. Russians will be able to openly embrace the object of desire that they have so far enjoyed in brief stolen moments. In fact, while I was in Moscow an event took place that might be construed as the first step toward making a legal union out of what has too often been an illicit affair: an American-managed bookstore opened for business, its stock available to any citizen with the right amount of cash. Years of pitched battle between American publishers and Soviet administrators seemed to have come to an end.

But when I visited the store, I saw it was perhaps not yet time for hosannas. The store is on the Krasnopresnenskaya Embankment out along the Moscow River, in a section of town that is far off the beaten track; there's not going to be any walk-in trade here. Nor is there much of a sense of welcome when you finally zero in on the target. There is a man sitting at the entrance politely inquiring about your intentions. That was standard operating procedure for years when the government didn't want citizens poking their noses in someplace—no barricades, no policemen, just a quiet little man noting down your name. Most Russians got the point and stayed away. This being the age of *glasnost,* probably there was nothing sinister about the man at the bookstore's door, but it is not the sort of thing that would put Muscovites at ease.

Also, shades of yesteryear, the American who had been designated manager had at the last moment been denied a visa. A pleasant Russian woman in her thirties was filling in. She proudly showed me newspaper clippings about the store's opening, and smiled modestly when I remarked that the headlines suggested the millennium had arrived. Then she graciously escorted me on a short tour. The books were indeed all here, from Salinger to Heller, all the volumes that till recently would have been impossible to find. Nevertheless, the store lacked any air of a celebratory breakthrough. There were only two other customers, and they had the look more of bureaucrats than lovers of the written word. The harsh lighting and the industrial-type steel shelving implied impermanency, a suggestion that with a change of policy everything could be quickly packed away once more and carried off into the night.

"Do you have Hemingway?" I asked.

"Of course."

"Do you have *For Whom the Bell Tolls?*" I asked.

"I'm not positive, but I think it is on the shelf."

It probably was. With the publication of Solzhenitsyn's collected diatribes against Soviet communism an imminent event, having *For Whom the Bell Tolls* is not worth exclaiming over. But it's worth a footnote. The book's career in Russia has been marked by deep love and sudden separation, by secret manuscripts and villainous authority—in other words, the usual story of American literature in Russia, though writ a bit larger than usual. The problem now is to find a satisfying ending to this story. Getting the book on the shelves may not be enough; it could use the cultural equivalent of a good hard scrubbing, to get rid of the incrustation of irrelevant meanings it has picked up over the years.

Up to the end of the 1930s, the authorities had tolerated Hemingway: to the extent any political position could be picked out, he seemed somewhere on the left. But a more explicit declaration of allegiances was required. The Spanish Civil War was the acid test. Hemingway's decision to join the Republicans seemed a favorable sign, an indication of a more mature socialist perspective; but the book that came out of that experience—*For Whom the Bell Tolls*—provoked official anger.

The novel contains several passages that are less than complimentary to the Russians who fought with the Republicans. The Russians congregated, we are told, in Gaylord's, a hotel in Madrid "that seemed too luxurious" and where "the food was too good for a besieged city, and the talk too cynical for a war." Hemingway offers this ironic explanation of the Gaylord's incongruous luxury: "But why shouldn't the representatives of a power that ruled a sixth of the world have a few comforts?" These and a few similar passages proved too much for an organization of Soviet veterans of the Spanish Civil War, and they published an open letter accusing Hemingway of slander. In truth the Russians play a tiny role in the novel, and one of them is portrayed as a paragon of bravery. Hemingway's ideological sins appear slight by any commonsensical standard, hardly justification for literary excommunication. That, however, is just the point: censorship in Russia was odious precisely because it was so whimsical. A chance remark led to literary oblivion, an unhappy metaphor to prison. Legend has it that Stalin read a translation of *For Whom the Bell Tolls* and glossed it thus: "Interesting. Publication forbidden." Of course no one would have argued.

Censorship cramped Russian intellectual life, but perhaps even worse is that it spread a sense of randomness. It was not only that some books were suddenly declared out of bounds, though that was bad enough. As disorienting was that the forbidden literature sometimes remained available, though it was impossible to predict where it would turn up. Such randomness had a long history. In Tsar Alexander's day, even high government officials routinely read contraband issues of the outlawed *Kolokol (The Bell)* in which London-based radicals called for revolution. In Brezhnev's day, when American newspapers were similarly forbidden, you could nevertheless get a copy of *The International Herald Tribune* just by going up to the right newsstand at the right time of day. During a year that I spent in Leningrad, an organization called International Communications Agency (ICA = CIA?) shipped in great quantities of books to Americans with the understanding that we would distribute them to Soviet friends; Solzhenitsyn and Trotsky, among others, passed through customs without arousing a murmur. The public libraries had hidden archives, special reserves, numbered limited editions that were stored away in carefully locked vaults, all of which was open to inspection under the right (never fully defined) conditions. In such a world, opinion about American literature was usually less a consequence of a step-by-step understanding than of luck, accident, and such happenstance as finding an acquiescent librarian. Is it any wonder that some Russians considered Meredith Wilson a major writer, and compared Salinger to Melville?

Hemingway was subjected to the full force of this randomness. During World War II, he was effectively in oblivion, though a few devotees kept the flame from dying out altogether. After the war his official status was upgraded to a gray area that made him neither totally forbidden nor totally acceptable. Sometimes reviews of his books appeared but not the book itself. Editions popped up in strange places—one novel bore the imprint of Detgiz, a publisher of children's literature. The journal *Inostrannaya literatura (Foreign Literature)* at first intended to publish *The Old Man and the Sea* but changed its plans because of rumors that Foreign Minister Vyacheslav Molotov disapproved; at a reception, Molotov was gingerly approached by one of the journal's editors. "I did not forbid publication," he said. "I did not read the book. I was told it was foolish. You decide for yourselves." Hemingway's career seemed to teeter in the winds of each day's news. He gained his widest readership in 1968 when a three-volume edition of his works was published with a run of 200,000, but even here the fragility of his career was palpable: two weeks later the Red Army invaded Czechoslovakia and Soviet society slipped into another long deep freeze. If publication had been slightly delayed, the collection would not have seen the light of day for another ten years or so.

All these contingencies added to Hemingway's allure; he seemed a writer heroically at odds with the lockstep march of Soviet history. But there was a cost. His image was continually displaced, redesigned, set in unfamiliar contexts. To many Russians, he seems a writer of the 1960s, which is when he escaped from extended oblivion; but of course by that time his talent was actually on the decline. The best of his works had been written many years before, and their references—fiestas, cosmopolitan bars, yachts—seemed anachronistic. Russians were aware that a more down-home sensibility, such as was represented by Cheever, Updike, and especially Salinger, defined contemporary America. It is only a slight exaggeration to say that Hemingway became popular and passé simultaneously.

The Russian version of *For Whom the Bell Tolls,* the book that started all of Hemingway's problems, was finally published as part of the 1968 three-volume edition, but even in his most forgiving mood the censor could not pass it without changes. A few of the passages about Gaylord's Hotel were cut or altered. The changes are slight and hardly affect the quality of the novel, but they have a significance nevertheless: they are thumbprints left by the censor, indications to the reading public that the authorities had riffled the pages before giving the book their stamp of approval. For Russian readers, who can't but be conscious of the wayward path *For Whom the Bell Tolls* took to get into their hands, the book can seem to be as much about Hemingway's battle against the Soviet bureaucracy as about Robert Jordan's fight against Franco's Falange.

"Hemingway became the most loved Soviet writer," said Kornei Chukovsky, an expert on American literature. This is hyperbole, but some sort of act of expropriation had indeed taken place. "Kheminguey," it is clear, is something very different from "Hemingway." Every country reads foreign authors in its own terms, but what the Russians have done with Hemingway goes beyond this norm: his literary corpus seems to have lost more than its original body weight of meaning, so that what remains is virtually a new entity altogether. At this point it is not enough simply to make Hemingway fully available; an errata slip should be added to each book, setting forth the cultural misapprehensions readers should try to avoid—except that it might run as long as the text itself. The bookstore on the Krasnopresnenskaya Embankment, despite the high hopes attending its opening, seems like a candle held up against a dark night sky. The night itself has yet to give way to a pervasive commonplace light.

On my way back from the bookstore, I made a small detour. Friends had been urging me to have a look at the Arbat, a street which has recently been converted into a pedestrian plaza. There were a couple of cozy-looking bookstores and well-stocked antique stores, and even a food stand with a couple of benches, an unusual amenity in this city which has so few urban graces that discomfort seems an official policy. Street musicians and artists were plying their crafts. I saw a man collecting signatures for a petition against political corruption. It reminded me of New York's Columbus Avenue minus the anxiety.

Near the center of the plaza a cluster of twenty or so people had gathered around a young man playing the guitar. The tune was familiar. It was Bob Dylan's "Blowin' in the Wind," and the young man was an American, with beard and in leather jacket, and with an upturned hat on the sidewalk in front of him. That was in some ways the greatest surprise—Moscow has never been a hospitable stop for the footloose young traveler. He sang with his eyes closed, a caricature of the artist in the throes of creation. At the end of each line, he paused, seemingly searching for inspiration. I considered singing along, to show the onlookers that the words had in fact long ago become common property. But then I decided to move on. Let the image remain as it was, I thought: a score or so of Russians, listening in rapt attention to what they thought was the latest news from America. What purpose would have been served in revealing that the bulletin was more than a decade late? American culture has arrived in a pell-mell style, and few Russians seem to care to take the time to sort it out properly.

I decided the time had come to contact Georgi Anzhaparidze, the editor-in-chief of the publishing house Khudozhestvennaya literatura. While still in America, I had heard him on National Public Radio discussing a short-story collection of Soviet and American writers to be jointly published by his firm and Knopf. The interviewer pressed him to admit that Soviet literature was inevitably distorted by ideological influences. He was never less than gracious, but he didn't give an inch, reminding her that American society exerted pressures of its own. How many authors write according to their conscience, he asked, and how many with an eye on a Hollywood movie sale? He seemed knowledgeable and undogmatic, an atypical combination for someone in the Soviet establishment, and I telephoned him at his Moscow office with a sense of anticipation. When I explained my interests, he invited me to come round to chat. That was the phrase he used; his letter-perfect, Oxford-accented English was honed in London, where he lived for several years.

Khudozhestvennaya literatura was on Novo-Basmannaya Street, a few uncomplicated blocks from the Lermontov metro stop. Despite Anzhaparidze's careful directions, however, I walked past the offices the first time around, failing to notice the minuscule sign. Inside the dank and gloomy lobby, there was an old woman sitting in a porter's booth; not raising her eyes from the newspaper in front of her, she motioned me up the decrepit stairs. A receptionist waved at me to come in without interrupting a phone conversation about grocery shopping. There was an air of dishevelment, out of place, I thought, in one of the country's major publishing houses.

But Anzhaparidze's inner office dispelled that impression. With its plush upholstered chairs and a large board-meeting sized table and luxurious carpets, it had the feel of a London club. Apparently, along with his accent, Anzhaparidze had picked up from the English a taste for the better things in life.

Tall, elegantly dressed, in his early fifties, he greeted me warmly. I could have been an old friend instead of a stranger who had called out of the blue. He directed me to a chair and offered a cigarette. Then, waving aside my Russian and shifting into his remarkable English, he launched into a nonstop, virtuoso explication of the meaning of American literature. On the contemporary situation he was direct. "There is really no one around now with the stature of Faulkner or Hemingway, is there? Updike, yes, of course, and Thomas Flanagan is interesting. But in general, it's a time of decline. You have your problems, we have ours, isn't that true?" he asked, but his confident tone indicated the question was rhetorical.

Barely noticing his secretary, who brought in a tea service— silver tray, gold-leaf cups, porcelain bowls with chocolate candies—Anzhaparidze expatiated without pause, carried along on the gusts of his own argument. He framed interrogatives, but didn't wait for my replies. "Which American authors are most read in Russia today? Recently one journal printed *Airport* and its circulation shot way up. I'm not proud of that fact, but neither is it a great shame, given the way the world is. What book has sold the most copies in your country? *Gone With the Wind*." He rolled his eyes in broad caricature of indignation. "Well, look here, you eat these chocolates, even though you know it's not good for your health. Life is not all duty. Literature is not all high art."

He got up and strolled around the room as if he needed more space to contain his energy. "Of course we have our little quirks in Russia, things that strike a foreigner as silly. But you have your quirks too. For example, those creative-writing classes in American colleges. We have absolutely nothing like that here. To me it seems an absurd institution, though I've been told it works out fine. The rich students help to support the poor writers." He smiled exuberantly, without malice. "Literature takes different forms in different places."

Pausing just a bit to consider, he offered his opinion of reading tastes in the two countries. "You know ideological correctness is no longer the test here. We'll print any American work that is good. But that does not mean we make no moral judgments—we want no pornography, no racism. You know my favorite recent American novel? *Something Happened* by Joseph Heller. It reminds me of Gorky's *Klim Sangin*. Perhaps I'm old-fashioned, but I like realism, and sometimes I find that American novelists do it as well as some of our classic writers. Heller and Gorky are in the same tradition, say what you will. You want to know my theory? The Russian mentality is most like the Quaker mind. We are a bit conservative, concerned about moral values."

He talked for an hour, until through the window I could see the evening coming on. I had come here in my role as observer of Russian habits but had stayed for the pleasure of listening to strong opinions expressed with gusto. Some spark of congeniality had been struck. "Listen," he told me, "you should come for dinner at my home one night. We need more time to get to the bottom of these thorny matters of American and Russian culture. I could send my car for you at your hotel—I have a chauffeur, you know." His tone suggested he found such pomp a bit ridiculous, more fitting for a head of state than a man of letters.

As I was leaving, Anzhaparidze had given me a recent translation of Dashiell Hammett's works, and on the metro ride back to my hotel I glanced through it. By way of an afterword, Anzhaparidze had written a long essay that, among other things, explained the "hard-boiled detective genre," put the *Smart Set* into its cultural context, and defined Hammett's idiosyncratic, wise-alecky tone. At the back of the volume there was a glossary of slang terms like "Mickey Finn," "Easy Street," and "rickey" (which I had forgotten was a lime-flavored drink). The book, like Anzhaparidze in person, had the knowing manner of someone who has assimilated his subject fully. It did not matter that his view of American literature was not the view of most Americans—at least he put our culture into a coherent shape.

Anzhaparidze was like Pushkin, I decided, a minor-league version but enough like him for the comparison to hold. In the first quarter of the nineteenth century, after the War of 1812 brought it abruptly into contact with Western Europe, Russia had endured the same sort of cultural influx it was suffering through now. Up through the end of the eighteenth century, Russia had been virtually isolated from foreign influence; it was suddenly faced with the task of making up for lost time as quickly as possible, and in this enterprise Pushkin was crucial. More than only a great poet, he was a great arbiter of culture. In the space of a decade or so he found native forms to accommodate every European trend from classicism to realism, thus making them comprehensible to the Russian mind. Now, with the new opening to the West, and to America especially, Russia again needs a Pushkin. No replicas being in sight, men of somewhat diminished stature like Anzhaparidze will have to bend to the task he once performed.

How many will it take to push the massive wheel of culture that Pushkin deftly manipulated by himself? How many Anzhaparidzes equal a Pushkin? Ten? Twenty? The numbers are daunting, especially since the Soviet Union has not been exactly a seedbed for imaginative thinking. There are other obstacles as well. The culture of Pushkin's day was circumscribed—in the course of a St. Petersburg soiree, one could meet virtually everyone who mattered. Today culture is fragmented, dispersed, fractured, and chance encounters on the Arbat can influence Russian minds as powerfully as the efforts of an important publisher.

Still, I decided, Russia should be cheered that Anzhaparidze was on the job. I recalled his invitation to dinner, and especially his merry offer to provide his chauffeured car. Not many Soviets in positions of power will joke about the perquisites of their office; the tough climb up the political ladder has left them humorless. Anzhaparidze seemed of an unusual cast, someone who had decided that life was a game in which you might as well enjoy the cards you have been dealt. A sense of the absurd backed by hard knowledge—that seemed a good formula for comprehending the American culture flooding through Russia's suddenly permeable borders.

Of the many observations I heard about America, among the least interesting were from someone who had been there. Vyacheslav Artyomev spent a year as composer-in-residence with the Las Vegas Symphony. He had hardly seen the garish downtown, had entered no casinos, and had no lasting impression of the surrounding desert landscape. His fondest memory, he told me, was of the Alpha Beta Supermarket. It was open round the clock, which meant he could work at his music uninterruptedly; he made clear that he did not like to worry about physical sustenance until his muse departed for the day.

Artyomev's view of his compositions was an unsettling mixture of the impersonal and the egocentric. His "Incantation," he has said, is "the resurrection of supra-individuality through the vehicle of the memory of genius." Artyomev may or may not have been a genius, but he certainly carried himself like one. His tousled hair and unkempt beard rising toward his cheekbones gave him the intense look of a man peering through a helmet visor. He spoke in an abrupt, sullen manner that suggested it pained him to give away valuable knowledge so easily. "To write music you have to know suffering, but suffering is in the mind of the artist, not something you see in the street," he informed me, even though I had not asked. Many of his statements were dicta only slightly disguised as conversation. We sat in his living room, which was dominated by a huge piano. His wife brought in tea, then meekly retired at his nod. "American music is naive, because Americans have not suffered," Artyomev announced. As the afternoon wore on, I increasingly felt closed in upon, pressed by his imperious ego.

Though Artyomev's words conveyed few hard facts to grab hold of, his manner reminded me of something worth bearing in mind. Russians are ardent believers in the special privileges of high art; Artyomev's posturing constituted an accepted national exercise.

Though contrary to all common sense, the nineteenth-century rig-marole about the artist's unique vision is still widely accepted. The thought that geniuses walk among them comforts Russians, pre-sumably because it suggests that at least a few individuals have managed to rise above the pervasive chaos. Once an artist has been designated a genius he can do no wrong; lesser creative efforts are greeted with no less praise than masterpieces—they are still the manifestations of a great spirit, even if one that is temporarily off its game. American artists tend to get categorized in the same way. Charlie Chaplin is a genius, which means he is a genius now and forever. His maudlin later films are admired as much as his earlier ones. Van Cliburn is another who has passed into the charmed circle, his twenty-year inactivity excused as a reasonable period of rest after heroic achievements.

Once in Leningrad, out in a desolate neighborhood by the Fin-land Bay, I noticed Stanley Kramer's *It's a Mad, Mad, Mad, Mad World* playing at a local movie theater in a dubbed version. I went in, mainly to find some relief from the cold but also to see how the Borscht Belt comedian Buddy Hackett would sound with Rus-sian coming out of his mouth. But when I later tried to describe this hilarious phenomenon to my Russian friends, they would not listen. They insisted on discussing the film's insights into the human condition. Stanley Kramer is a director who has been designated a genius—he can do no less than direct masterpieces.

Believing in the mysteries of high art, Russians might have been inclined to scorn American mass culture, but in fact it's one of their great weaknesses. They have always had a taste for our more ram-bunctious art forms, our most down-and-dirty styles. The cake-walk was the rage in St. Petersburg society almost as soon as in Harlem, and American popular music has had a loyal following ever since. Interest in jazz held fast even during the bleak Stalin years, with many hotels and restaurants featuring a *dzhaz* (jazz band). In 1935, *The New York Times* correspondent reported that "one Moscow hotel has an American Negro tap dancer who nightly brings down the house," and the Hotel Metropol kept its dance floor open for jazz devotees until three in the morning. As for American pulp fiction, Russians are addicted. At the turn of the century, detective heroes like Nick Carter and Nat Pinkerton were so popular that a term was coined to describe the phenomenon: *pinkertonovshchina*. Russians liked the thrill of the chase, but they seemed to like still more the peculiarly American hero, hard-boiled and ruthlessly just. In one of the Russian versions of this genre, Nick Carter triumphs over the criminals "by throwing their bodies into the sewer, which was intended for garbage and all sorts of muck. . . . 'That's the way we deal with such dirty criminals in the U.S.,' he announces." At the beginning of the century, it was detective stories; now it is Harold Robbins and Arthur Hailey. They absorb it all eagerly. Rock and roll, Western movies, poster art— Russians are insatiable for our low art, and the lower the better.

To worship at the shrine of Parnassus while enjoying shoot-'em-ups requires a bit of mental juggling. Russians manage by keeping the categories of high and low art rigorously distinct. Certain cultural items bear an imaginary label warning the consumer—"do not confuse this with high art or it may be dangerous to your aesthetic taste." No crossover is tolerated, no mixing of genres. I attended a performance of the Alvin Ailey dance company when it was on its Russian tour, watching with pleasure as they mixed ballet and softshoe to the music of Duke Ellington and Charles Ives. The audience was nonplussed. The woman next to me turned to her neighbor and said, "It's some sort of gymnastics set to music." She wasn't condescending, and indeed was soon applauding enthusiastically. The Alvin Ailey company wasn't the Kirov, but once that was established it could be enjoyed for what it was.

The high-low schema has served for a long time, but it has lately exhibited some signs of strain in its application to America. Our cultural climate of late modernism and early shoddiness has produced a breakdown in the traditional hierarchies of the arts, and genius is now obviously just a costume that artists wear to work. In America we've perforce gotten used to this disorder, but Russians have not. In fact, many of them would be happy to lop off our cultural development somewhere around 1960, that time when true artists seemed to have an indisputable lineage and true works of art seemed to shine with a distinctive glow. The Soviet Union must be one of the few places in the world where it's still possible to hear a serious discussion about the genius of Sinclair Lewis or Rockwell Kent. But there is a growing sense that this misses the point.

The Soviet Union's establishment has now begun willy-nilly to try to come to terms with the new truths of American culture. The official line used to be that American popular art was kitsch or philistine whimsy, either way deserving only disdain. Now a new category has been devised for art that rises above the trivial but still falls short of the highest purpose. Into this category have been stuffed all manner of cultural objects, from Coppola's films to Warhol's paintings and Vonnegut's novels. Its main function, however, is to accommodate American popular music, which has become too influential with the young generation to be dismissed or laughed away.

Among the most prominent signs of the changing times is the stadium in Gorky Park. Till very recently the most boisterous music on that stage had been folk singers wielding mandolins, but now several hugely popular rock concerts have been permitted here, including several by American musicians. Though the stadium's official name is Zelyony Teatr (The Green Theater), many call it by the name of the adjoining building, the Hard Rock Café—a nod in the direction of the New York club scene that would have been unthinkable a few years ago. Some of my Russian friends scorned the Hard Rock complex, noting that cutting-edge rock music is to be found in Moscow only in certain out-of-the-way apartments and deserted factories, not in a government-subsidized entertainment center. But for me that was just the point, a measure of exactly how far the government would go to accommodate the influence of American pop culture.

A young musician took me on a tour of the complex, beginning with the café. It was filled with young people who in their dress, posture, and even manner of speech suggested to me that I had passed into another country. It was not yet the East Village, but neither was it the buttoned-up Soviet Union I had been used to. Volodya, my guide, had a manner I recognized from New York but had not seen much of here; reserved and self-aware, he moved like someone testing out a role. He treated me with determined nonchalance, as though waiting to see how well I would fit into his performance.

"You should have seen this place when Quincy Jones was here," he remarked, as we walked up the stairs. "Foreigners think Moscow is the provinces as far as rock music goes, but that isn't true anymore."

I mumbled the one or two facts I remembered about Quincy Jones and, for good measure, added a generality about the state of rock music in America. Volodya gave me a sharp look.

We entered a flashy high-tech recording studio. "Look at these tapes," Volodya said, motioning to the floor-to-ceiling shelves. "Anything you can hear in the States, you can hear right here."

I looked around, trying to appear knowledgeable. Volodya waited expectantly for a comment. When he saw I had none to offer, he shrugged with a show of weariness and led us forward.

We climbed to the upper reaches of the stadium and Volodya expatiated on the sophisticated sound system. I responded only with a remark about the lovely park setting, which earned me an exasperated snort from Volodya.

Soon after, Volodya became a bit more forthcoming. We never did have a conversation, but a few consecutive sentences were uttered. He had apparently sized me up to his satisfaction and decided that there was no point in striking a pose before someone with my abysmal musical taste. Relaxing a bit, he rattled off names that meant nothing to me but that he insisted were crucial to the modern sensibility: Captain Beefheart, Swans, Residents, Pere Ubu, Hot Tuna. If I wanted to see how these sounds all came together, he said, I should come to hear his group in concert later that week. He implied it would be for my own good.

I left the Hard Rock a bit stunned by the realization that these

Russians were more knowing about parts of American culture than I was. It didn't matter that I only listened to rock music when trapped in a traffic jam; in the old days, even meager knowledge of an aspect of American life qualified you as an expert in Russia— in the land of the blind, the one-eyed man is king, and in the land of the culturally dispossessed so is the man who has tuned in to New York's FM stations a couple of times. I decided to attend Volodya's concert, if only to see precisely how out of date this bit of folk wisdom had become.

The concert's venue, it turned out, was a highly appropriate place for gauging the state of popular culture in Russia. The Manège, which was once the tsar's riding academy and now houses the Museum of Contemporary Art, is the site of a famous confrontation between those who would bring innovative art to Russia and those who were having none of it. During an exhibit in 1962, Nikita Khrushchev stood in front of a few mildly avant-garde paintings and sculptures and pronounced them unequivocal *govno* (shit), adding a few other choice expletives culled from his country-boy past. That outburst drove a stake into the heart of Russia's innovative art movement, and simultaneously brought a short-lived cultural thaw to a halt.

The current exhibit showed how far Russia has come since then; innovative art, it turns out, did not die at Khrushchev's hand. Cartoon art, mobiles, clothes designed like sculpture: these were some of the items on display that defied the old Socialist Realist tenets. One painting—which drew the biggest crowd—was entitled *Red Square in Summer* and showed demonstrators marching in front of Lenin's Tomb holding aloft protest posters. The painting's content was remarkable for a public exhibition in the Soviet Union, but its style was even more interesting. It resembled the old Socialist Realism, but had a slight cartoonish flavor. It was an attack from within, a use of the Socialist Realist method in order to render it absurd.

Looking around, I noted that Volodya and three other musicians were mounting the makeshift stage at one end of the huge hall. They took a long time setting up, chatting and moving around and smoking and in general behaving as if making music was the last thing on their minds. A few people sat down on folding chairs in front of the stage, but most kept circulating around the hall, hardly aware that a concert was about to begin. But the music, once begun, was of the sort that could not be ignored. It was like a wave of dissonance from which there was no escape. Occasionally a melody tried to struggle forward, but then would fall back in exhaustion into the sea of noise. Almost everyone reacted with undisguised dislike; some ostentatiously contorted their faces as if in pain. A few days later Volodya told me that the museum attendants had written a letter of protest, threatening to resign if that sort of music was ever permitted there again. He found their reaction uproariously funny.

For me, the episode had been an opportunity to measure the cultural moment. Many Russians have apparently reached the stage where they will tolerate the innovative; but the very innovative leaves them cold. The paintings and sculpture in the exhibit, though in a style several neighborhoods of the mind removed from the Socialist Realism that once held sway, were still familiar. But there are many stages to pass through, many areas of taste to be tamed, before the average Russian will accept the sensibility that spawned Captain Beefheart.

I remembered one particular visitor to the exhibit, a woman who looked old enough to have lived through a couple of the ice ages that have afflicted Soviet cultural history. She stared at the paintings as if transfixed, hardly moving; she might have been praying, so passionate was her concentration. I was watching her when Volodya's group struck its first notes, and she hardly looked up. She simply put her hands to her ears—not angrily or maliciously, but distractedly—and moved on to the next canvas in that awkward posture. She just did not have the energy to take everything in at once.

• • •

The American popular art that Russians have loved most un-reservedly is movies. As early as the 1920s, American movies had captured the public's fancy. Most were of less than edifying nature ("A poem of human passion in two parts and fourteen reels" said the 1929 advertisement in *Pravda* for MGM's *Sodom and Gomorrah*) and the government was not pleased. When Eisenstein's great film *Battleship Potemkin* was finished in 1926, it was immediately hauled into the battle—here was a chance at last to turn Soviet audiences away from philistine American films. No effort was spared. The Moscow theater where *Potemkin* opened was decorated to resemble a battleship, and the staff was dressed up like members of the crew. There was broad advertising. But it was not to be. Audiences preferred Douglas Fairbanks in *Robin Hood,* which had been released at about the same time; the MGM adventure tale was so popular that it had to be installed in eleven of the twelve first-run cinemas in the center of Moscow. After *Potemkin* had an unexpected success in Berlin, another effort was made to build it into a popular hit at home. But two weeks after its rerelease, it was removed from the screen, replaced by Buster Keaton's *Our Hospitality* and "back by popular demand" (according to *Pravda*), Fairbanks in *Robin Hood* once again.

Russian audiences doted upon Hollywood stars. The visit of Fairbanks and Mary Pickford to Moscow caused so much excite-ment that a commemorative pamphlet entitled "They Are Here" ["*Oni u nas*"] was published in an edition of 45,000 copies. A 1927 Soviet film entitled *The Kiss of Mary Pickford, or The Story of how Douglas Fairbanks and Igor Ilyinsky quarreled because of Mary Pickford* was hugely popular. It tells of a luckless young man with a dreary job and no future who is changed into a popular and happy hero; the transforming event is a kiss from Mary Pickford, and there were many watching in the movie theaters of Russia who would have believed she possessed such power.

In subsequent years, Russians found other Hollywood stars to admire. Jimmy Stewart, Henry Fonda, Spencer Tracy, Bette Davis are all well-known here. Several of my Russian friends still lapse into dreamy nostalgia when they recall watching John Wayne in action. His *Stagecoach* (seized by the Red Army from German archives at the end of World War II) was always shown with an added commentary running over the opening credits—audiences were instructed to note how cruelly American cowboys treated the native Indians. But at the moment of the dramatic shoot-out, everyone rooted for Wayne's Cisco Kid.

Quite a few Russians seem to believe that their long-standing affection for American movies, maintained in the face of government disapproval, has earned them certain proprietary rights. They put forward their critical opinions with an insider's confidence, and do not like to be contradicted by foreigners, not even Americans. Walt Disney always seems to lead to an argument. I think of him as a pretty good cartoonist with an unfortunate sadistic streak. To Russians he is a genius. (He was first certified thus by Eisenstein.) As it happened, I got to see their admiration for Disney in full flower, since my stay in Moscow coincided with a festival commemorating the sixtieth birthday of Mickey Mouse.

Disney was popular all through the 1930s, but beginning after World War II there was a long period when the cartoons were not shown. I had heard stories that they had been taken off the screen because they were judged to promote the capitalist ideology. Luck provided me with an opportunity to check these stories at the source. On the morning of the festival's opening I ran into Roy Disney, the great man's son, in the hotel dining room, and I asked him if in fact Donald Duck had been condemned as a running dog of capitalism. He laughed. "The only reason the cartoons weren't shown is that there was a disagreement about copyright payments. Donald Duck obviously has no ideology," he assured me, and turned back to discussing with his wife and cronies the merits of the plumbing in hotels around the world. From what I overheard, it seemed that they had put the National near the bottom of the list.

I invited the daughter of a Russian friend to go with me to the gala opening of the festival—I thought that Maya's five-year-old perspective might help me to get into the spirit of the occasion. To get to the theater on Pushkin Square, we had to travel on both bus and metro, a trip of almost an hour. On the way, I tried to explain Mickey Mouse and Donald Duck to her, but she wasn't interested. She wanted me to read the book she had brought with her, Marshak's *The Leningrad Postman,* a great favorite with Russian children. With each stanza detailing the adventures of this dedicated civil servant, Maya grew more comfortable and affable. The recurrent refrain—*Leningradskii pochtalyon/Leningradskii pochtalyon*—soothed her. By the time we reached our stop she had curled herself against me and was calling me *dyadya* (uncle), and the other passengers were smiling at us with approval.

There was a gala air inside the theater. Looking around as we made our way to our seats, I was surprised to find that the audience was composed of more than only kids and their parents. A lot of adults had come on their own, presumably to honor the films that had enlivened their childhoods. A drumroll was heard and a burst of applause swept the hall as an actor dressed like Mickey Mouse walked onto the stage. Maya, I took note, did not applaud or smile.

There followed a round of speechmaking by Soviet officials, much of it hyperbolic to my ear. Mickey, it turned out, was not just a funny little rodent but a creature remarkable for his energy, sincerity, and openness—in fact, "an eternal hero." I stared at the costumed Mickey standing off modestly to the side and tried to summon up the qualities that had just been itemized, but it was no use. Everyone else in the audience, however, seemed well satisfied with the accuracy of the description; everyone, that is, except Maya, who stared morosely ahead.

Dapper in his blue blazer, white cuffs showing just the right amount, Roy Disney approached the microphone, waited for the applause to die away, and then spoke. "Wow," he said. It was pure show-biz, accepted L.A. code for expressing modesty while preening in the acclaim. The Russian audience was at first befuddled, and the translator, who had tried to find a native equivalent for Disney's exclamation, gave up in mid-effort. But after a pause, there was general applause. This was, after all, a genius's son. Maya put two of her fingers into her mouth and kept them there.

The lights finally dimmed and a circa 1940 Donald Duck cartoon appeared on the screen. *Donald Duck's Crime* it was called, and it showed how Donald, in order to finance a date with Daisy, steals the penny bank belonging to his nephews. Only the sight of his nephews kneeling by their bed to pray for the return of their money moves Donald to right the wrong he has done. In its mixture of greed and sentimental religiosity, it struck me as a pretty odd choice for a festival in the Union of Soviet Socialist Republics; maybe Donald's long banning had been for cause after all. The audience, however, took it in blandly, and waited patiently for the program to proceed. A festival official approached the lectern and announced that the evening's main feature, Disney's classic movie *Fantasia,* would follow immediately, and the audience settled back with palpable anticipation. Maya, I noted, had taken her fingers out of her mouth and was playing with the buttons on her sweater. Her face had taken on an expression of distaste. As the credits for *Fantasia* began to roll and the Stokowski score kicked in, Maya started to cry, soft sobs at first and then a bit louder. She wouldn't tell me what was wrong. I tried to calm her, but she was having none of that. She wanted to leave, and after she kicked her shoes away into the next row I gave in.

By the time we reached the metro, she had stopped crying, but had turned irascible. She refused my hand and paid no attention to my directions. To make matters worse, I found that my Russian was getting wobbly. It had gotten me through complex discussions on economics and art, but calming a querulous five-year-old on public transportation was a new test. I needed not words but a tone—firm but affectionate—and it eluded me. I limited myself to one-word commands, which upset Maya all the more.

Annoyed by the whole business, I let my attention wander during the transfer from metro to bus, and I boarded us onto the 101 instead of the 103. By the time I realized my mistake, we had plunged into the inky gloom of a huge industrial park. Responding to my question, a fellow passenger roused himself from an alcoholic sleep long enough to grunt out the information that the bus would loop back toward my destination. Ten minutes passed and I still did not see any familiar landmarks. Maya, who had lapsed into glum silence, must have picked up on my anxiety, for she began to cry once more. The other passengers began looking meaningfully in our direction.

Desperate, I took out *The Leningrad Postman* and began to read. *Leningradskii pochtalyon/Leningradskii pochtalyon*—to my surprise, the recurrent refrain seemed to calm Maya almost instantly, and she cuddled up against me exactly as she had on the inward bound trip. The change was so abrupt, it seemed more chemical than psychological, and Marshak may, for all I know, be the medically approved antidote to Disney. Donald Duck had infected Maya with his manic criminality; a dose of a civil servant's punctiliousness was just what the doctor ordered. Sometimes, native ways are the best ways.

As a five-year-old, Maya was a bit of a brat, but as a cultural critic she had her good points. She was, I saw with grudging respect, hard to take in. The audience in the Pushkin Theater had accepted without argument every aspect of Walt Disney that had been paraded before them, from the son's Hollywood hype to the cartoon extolling the virtues of saving and praying. They were not going to give up their idealized Disney just because the actual version fell on its face. But Maya, unhampered by preconception, had known capitalist trash when she saw it.

Perhaps the old saw about the dangers of ignoring the past deserves a footnote in today's Russia; ignoring the past may sometimes be the best of the available approaches. Many of the Russians I watched as they confronted America kept tripping over old events. The example of my five-year-old companion suggested that acting as if this was Day One in American-Russian relations might have something to be said for it—honesty, for one thing. Too bad, I told myself, that this choice was probably open only to those, like Maya, who have never heard the tales about America that have been repeated so often no one stops to think very deeply about them.

# six

# Passionate Etiquettes

As with many legends, the legend of how Isadora Duncan met Sergei Esenin has several versions. Witnesses' accounts differ; rumor has been added for spice and dollops of hearsay stirred into the broth. But all the versions agree that the encounter between the American dancer and the Russian poet was a meeting of star-crossed lovers, of individuals so passionately drawn to each other that they did not even need a common language.

When Duncan came on tour to Russia in 1921, she was already the toast of Europe. Her dancing was acclaimed, her private life a matter of intense curiosity. She was a star. Esenin was a young bohemian poet with a growing reputation in Russia, and a taste for bigger things. Three accounts of their first meeting fix the location in an artist's studio in Moscow, shortly after Duncan's arrival in the country. "Isadora reclined on a couch with Esenin at her feet. She plunged her hand into his curls and said '*Zolotaya golova* [golden head].'" This version displays a certain awareness of its myth-making tendencies, since it goes on to remark that "It was surprising that she, who knew no more than a dozen Russian words, knew precisely these two." Later that evening, we are told, Duncan kissed Esenin and—still relying on her small but amazingly appropriate stock of Russian—called him "*chort* (devil)." A second version has fewer words and more action. "Suddenly the door burst open and the most beautiful face she claimed ever to have seen, crowned with golden glittering curls, and with piercing blue eyes, stared into hers. She needed no introduction. She opened her arms, and he fell on his knees clasping her close to him, shouting 'Isadora, Isadora, mia mia.' " A third account, the most sober-sided, claims that Duncan's first words were in English and somewhat less than enthusiastic. "Who is this youth with such a depraved face?" she asked. All the versions indicate that the dancer and the poet became lovers that first night.

The subsequent marriage did not live up to such glorious beginnings. Reality intruded. She was forty-four and he was twenty-five. The differences in their fame galled Esenin; during their 1922–23 tour of America, he grew more and more angry at how little attention was directed his way. When drunk, which was often, he became arrogant, self-pitying, and argumentative. She was always adept at the grand gesture, but not much good at marital routines. They separated less than two years after they met, and by then things had already been going downhill for some time. A narrative faithfully detailing the course of their time together would make for melancholy reading; only by concentrating on the brilliant beginnings is it possible to construct a legend, a legend of souls instantaneously joining.

It is as a legend that the Duncan-Esenin affair can serve as inspiration for a recent tendency in Russian-American relations: people-to-people diplomacy. The idea has been around for a while, but it has only lately assumed its present extravagant proportions. Numerous citizen exchanges have been organized; so-called "telebridges" (Russians and Americans talking directly via satellite transmission) have been broadcast several times; and a number of communities in the two countries have declared themselves "sister cities," pledging fidelity with all the enthusiasm of siblings reunited after long separation. The assumption underlying these encounters is comparable to the dramatic logic of the Duncan-Esenin legend:

if we could only meet on a truly personal basis, free of the burdens of nationality, we could understand each other perfectly. We are all alike under our cultural skin, men and women driven by the same human needs, like Esenin and Duncan, though on not so grand a scale.

Presumably there is some truth to this idea. One hopes so. But experience suggests that people tend to feel uncomfortable discarding their cultural skins and running around in their naked humanity. National characteristics ease the blankness of existence. Indeed, even if it were somehow to circumvent all differences regarding economics and ideology and art, each nation would probably insist that only it had mastered the correct way of handling knives and forks. Though the etiquettes of living—including the etiquette of love—are nowhere written down, they have the force of law.

It therefore pays to have a story to set against the Duncan-Esenin legend, some cautionary tale for the benefit of those who put their stock in the glories of one-to-one encounters. The travels of American literary critic Edmund Wilson through the Soviet Union in 1932–34 will serve nicely. Ruthlessly analytic by nature, Wilson cast a cold eye on the idea that emotion could transport you beyond social circumstances. Throughout his trip he gathered evidence to counter the hope that Russian-American harmony was easily accessible. "Americans," he wrote, "who have decided, as I have done, that Americans and Russians are much alike, discover that in the ordinary technique of life, their habits are antipodally different." It was partly a matter of character, Russians tending to procrastinate where Americans acted decisively, Russians being imprecise where Americans were clear. It was also a matter of different codes governing daily life. "The Russians are funny about this," he noted of their swimming habits. "At the dacha from which we had started it was considered extremely improper to put on a bathing suit in the house and then walk to the river in them . . . What you were supposed to do here was to go down in your clothes to the river and get undressed in broad daylight on the bank, laying your clothes on the grass. Then you would put on your bathing suits if you had them, or, if not, just go in naked." Wilson was not smirking—his temperament inclined him to give full credit to foreign customs. Russians were not silly, they simply behaved in ways different from ours.

But for all his detached sociological air, even Wilson gave in to the dream that a Russian and American could achieve a meeting of souls. Since he was a man of famously goatish appetite, it's not surprising that Wilson did not imagine a romance in the style of Duncan and Esenin; but he did have a moment when he fully believed that the blind erotic urge would carry him beyond all the national differences he had himself carefully assessed. In a small town on the banks of the Volga, he met an attractive peasant girl, and very soon he became convinced that a spark of mutual attraction had been lit. He prepared for the expected outcome. "We sat gazing at each other. After a moment I began to pet her. I patted and stroked her cheeks and neck, and she sat looking straight at me with her frank and gentle eyes. This went on for a considerable time, but didn't seem to lead to anything, and I began to feel as if I was patting a pony. I stopped and said goodnight and went to bed."

The moment is worth preserving: a blank, unbridgeable abyss between two individuals who seemed on the verge of harmony. No matter how close Russians and Americans may at times seem, there is always the chance our respective cultural histories will rise up to divide us, denying us a full-blown empathy.

Encounters between individuals from different nations usually involve a staking out of home turf before there can be any exploration of common ground. But Russians guard their prerogatives even beyond the norm. This attitude is perhaps most visible in the treatment of foreigners on Russian soil. There is a tradition that goes back to the time of Peter the Great, who imported many foreign workers and technicians to help build the city of St. Petersburg; the local labor force was all right for hauling stones and digging ditches but lacked finer skills. The foreigners were well paid and comfortably housed in a section of town that acquired the name *Nemetskaya sloboda* (German Town). A considerable number of the foreigners were indeed German, but that does not adequately explain the reasoning behind the name. The word for "German," *Nemets,* is cognate with the word for "dumb," "incapable of speech"; Germans first of all, but also anyone else not speaking Russian was uttering sounds beneath the level of human interest. Even as Russians were forced to accept the aid of outsiders, they believed themselves essentially superior—a nervous superiority, never entirely sure of itself, but persistent. *Nemetskaya sloboda* was at one and the same time a privileged preserve and a place to quarantine an inferior way of life. That's been the style for centuries: receive foreigners royally, scrape and bow in their presence—but in taking what they have to offer, never let them fully into the native life. That paradise is reserved for Russians.

Russians' treatment of foreigners on their soil has often been colored by a particular form of xenophobia. Slavophilism, Pan-Slavism, The Black Hundreds, most lately the Pamyat movement have all had as a basic principle a belief in the purity of the Russian soul, a purity that must be kept safe from contamination from the West. It's to the point that Solzhenitsyn, who stands squarely in this tradition, has criticized Marxism as much for its European provenance as for its ideology. Like most xenophobias, Russia's has a bullying tone, but there is also a tacit admission of weakness. The Russian soul must be a very delicate thing if it can be infected by the slightest alien touch.

During most of the nineteenth century, these ambivalent attitudes toward visiting foreigners hardly affected Americans—few came to Russia, and those who did remained on the periphery of the life of the country. Entrepreneurs appeared periodically with grand plans (the grandest being a General Electric project for a telegraph line across the Bering Sea, through Siberia, and thence overland to Europe), but nothing came of these. American generals and weapons manufacturers like Samuel Colt negotiated arms deals with the Russian military establishment. Diplomats came and went, in most cases hardly venturing beyond court circles. A number of American singers and actors toured Russia to great acclaim (Ira Aldridge, a black Shakespearean, made a very big splash), but performers by definition were outside workaday society. For all these visiting Americans, Russia was an accidental backdrop for other concerns, not a society to live in; they looked at it as one might look at a tourist spectacle.

Indeed, the status of Americans in nineteenth-century Russia is very neatly reflected in the reactions of one American who did come as a tourist, Nathan Appleton, a distant relative of the poet Henry Wadsworth Longfellow. "One must pass the winter somewhere," he noted in his diary, "and why not here, where so few Americans have tried it?" He occupied himself with sleigh rides and balls and horse racing, finding the surroundings at best picturesque and sometimes downright comical. "Driving down the Nevsky [Prospect] from Moscow Station, St. Petersburg looked *so* funny," he noted in a letter home. After an afternoon visiting Kronstadt in the company of two other Americans, he declared, "The whole effect of the day and the adventures were eminently Russian." Though extreme in their callowness, Appleton's views reflect a general tendency among Americans to reduce Russia to scenery. They glided through, oblivious to the life around them, and for their part most Russians hardly noticed their presence.

The situation after the Revolution was very different. American workers and intellectuals came in the thousands, some staying on for years, and a few forever. Many played crucial roles in the rebuilding task. The most prominent example was Colonel Hugh Cooper (chief consultant on the Muscle Shoals dam), who helped supervise construction of the Dneproges power plant. But even when Americans performed less spectacularly, they constituted a presence that was noted and acknowledged. The economy was dotted with organizations and associations that had a recognizably American flavor: the California Flour Mill, the American Farming Commune and the Seattle Commune in the Caucasus, the Russian-American Factory in Moscow, the Astoria Fish Combine near Murmansk. The American community in Russia was sizable enough and coherent enough to support an English-language newspaper, *The Moscow News,* which at least at first was edited and written by Americans.

The government's policy was compounded of welcome and distrust, the latter predominating. It tried to make the life of American workers comfortable by providing goods not available to the local population and paying high salaries, sometimes in gold. At the same time, great efforts were made to keep the Americans from being absorbed into the daily life of the country. Whenever possible, they were made to work together in special groups; with only a few exceptions, they were barred from joining the trade unions and other associations; often they were quartered together in designated housing.

At Magnitogorsk, for example, American workers lived in a section known locally as "the American City." John Scott, who spent several years in Magnitogorsk and later became a journalist for *Life* noted: "The Americans played poker, read the *Saturday Evening Post,* and attempted to forget in their off-hours that they were in a Siberian waste on the other side of the world from home." Having the comforts of hot water and central heating while the Russian workers outside "the American City" had to make do with shanties must have made the Americans feel like lords above the rabble; but lords is not how the Russians considered them. It's no accident that "the American City" should recall Peter the Great's *Nemetskaya sloboda.* Revolutionary Russia treated the Americans with the same mixture of coddling and exploitation, hospitality and suspicion, that had animated tsarist policy.

There were some purely contemporary factors. Politics (unease about the allegiances of men and women who till lately had lived under capitalism) and administrative needs (attempts to impose order after the devastation of civil war) were not the same as in Peter's time. But it was Russia's bone-deep xenophobia that was probably the key factor—indeed, average citizens were as suspicious of Americans as the policymakers in Moscow. A *Moscow*

*News* correspondent, surveying the condition of American workers in Stalingrad and Kharkov, found that they were deeply resented. Soviet workers tried to avoid them. As much as possible the Americans were shunted off into the role of consultants who were not consulted.

Local resistance was even sharper in Kamerevo, home of Project Kuzbas. The natives occasionally refused to work under American supervision and once or twice went so far as to sabotage the machinery. The Americans must have seemed a slash on the landscape, an insult to national sensitivities. They had (on government advice) brought large supplies of food—butter, cheese, sardines—that was unavailable to the local population. They organized baseball games on the steppes. They married Russian women, in one case dressing the bride in American-style clothes. It was a no-holds-barred culture clash. When the Americans used formaldehyde against the insects infesting their homes, the Russians bitterly joked that their own homes were being overrun by cockroaches seeking refuge from foreign attack. It was a joke, but it captures the tenor of the situation: Americans seemed to be steamrolling their way through native life, altering its fabric on the most minute level.

In general, however, the nation's attitude was not so much anti-American as a what's-in-it-for-us cynicism. Americans were welcome as long as they could be put to some use. One of the characters in Valentin Kataev's novel *Time Forward* (1933) is an American engineer who has come to help with the construction of Magnitogorsk (residing, presumably, in "the American city"). The man has proven himself an invaluable worker even though his motives are dubious by Soviet standards; he wants to earn enough money to buy a house in some small American town to which he can retire. Catastrophe strikes when the stock-market crash wipes out his savings; stunned, the American drinks himself into a stupor and accidentally sets fire to his bed, killing himself. There is an ideological moral here—capitalism destroys capitalists—but it is Kataev's tone that is more interesting. Throughout the book the American has been treated respectfully, even affectionately, but he is sent to his death with absolutely no sympathy. The welcome Russia extended to Americans was highly contingent.

Visiting Russia in the 1970s and early 1980s, I enjoyed an array of privileges accruing from my nationality. At box offices where Russians waited for hours for tickets, Americans were encouraged to wave their passports and go right to the front of the line. If they were academics, they were given special seats in the libraries; if they were journalists, they were housed in comfortable quarters. Also, Americans could do their shopping in special stores where all manner of quality goods and foods not available elsewhere could be had for dollars. Though there was never a guard at the door, the locals understood these Beryozka stores were off-limits; those who tried to enter found themselves hustled quickly back onto the street.

In Leningrad once, I exited the Beryozka on Herzen Street feeling flush with the pleasures of a bargain purchase, and also, I admit, with the feeling of privilege. It's hard to deny the sense of exhilaration that comes from having access where others are forbidden. I was musing in this way as I turned onto Gogol Street, away from the crowds, when my thoughts were interrupted by the approach of three young men. It's a favorite sport among Soviet teenagers to hang around Beryozka stores and approach foreigners to ask the time of day. Any reply requires a grammatical construction beyond the capacity of most nonnative speakers, and the kids usually get the laugh they seek. But the four blocking my path did not have such a lark in mind. With their leather jackets and grim expressions, they seemed threatening, though what they were threatening I could not guess.

"Passport," demanded the tallest, while the other three assumed positions that might or might not have been designed to block my escape.

"For what reason?" I replied, regretting my ignorance of the law governing such occasions.

"*Militsya*," said one, using the term that can mean everything from police to neighborhood security group.

I glanced at the other three to see if their expression wouldn't give away the joke. Nothing of the sort was evident. For a moment I considered turning on my heel and walking away, daring them to take action; but what I in fact did was to produce my passport. They inspected it, grunted, returned it, and then departed. It had seemed easier to comply than to argue, but to be frank, fear played a role—why risk running afoul of an authority that could be implacably mean?

As the band of four turned the corner, I glimpsed them breaking into laughter and backslapping, and I realized I had been put in my place. My sense of privilege evaporated as if it had never existed. I had been made to realize that however much I was cosseted as an American with dollars to spend, it was Russians who made the rules here, all of them. I was in the country at Russian dispensation.

That was then; this is now—Gorbachev's Russia. Have attitudes changed? To gauge the new mood I would have liked to have looked up some of the Americans who had come in the 1920s and 1930s and then stayed on, but they are a quickly vanishing breed, hard to find, and so I settled for the next best thing. Paula Garb is the spiritual descendant of that earlier generation of Americans. She has written a book about their experiences, tracking down the survivors in remote corners of Russia. She has lived in Moscow for more than ten years. It's only a sign of the changing times that, unlike the Americans she has written about, Paula Garb came to Russia neither because of political principle nor a desire for a good payday; she fell in love with the Russian guide of her tour group.

On the telephone she gave me intricate directions to her home. "No matter how detailed I am, most visitors lose their way," she said. I had to ride out to the end of one of the metro lines, then take a bus, then walk for a bit. I proceeded with care, determined to prove to Garb that I should not be classed with the befuddled norm.

The bus took me through a bleak suburb. Across from my stop a green hill had been sliced through to reveal red-orange clay, the scar of some excavation apparently abandoned midway through the job. Six high-rise apartment buildings were grouped haphazardly to form an irregular courtyard with crumbling cement pathways and some sickly patches of grass. I found the right building and ascended to the twelfth floor, riding an elevator, which lurched and moaned as if in pain. I decided I had wandered into quintessential Russia, a never quite finished country.

An attractive woman of about forty opened the door in response to my ring, abruptly dispelling the Russian aura. Her manner was brisk, without the elaborate hospitality that I had grown used to these last weeks. Her hello included a bit of Stateside irony about how well I had navigated the course to her house. She led me into her study, which was furnished sparely with desk and bed-cum-sofa but had a commanding view back toward the city center. From the next room I heard the sounds of a Hitchcock movie. "My son," she said, noticing my curiosity. "We just got a VCR." I was reminded of her specialness, and also how little it takes here to affirm that specialness—one gets attuned to the smallest signs of privilege, automatically registering increments of material possession.

Over tea she told me her story. She was born and grew up near Denver, but had always felt out of place there. For one thing, her mother was an atheist, at that time and place still a social stigma. The Soviet Union always seemed to offer an alternative, however dimly she was able to imagine it. When in college, she took a tour to Moscow and Leningrad, and fell in love with the country—and with the tour guide. She eventually returned to stay, got married, had children, went to work at a publishing house, was divorced: an American woman's typical cycle, but lifted out of the ordinary by the setting.

"Men and women are on better terms here than in the United States. At my job there is perfect equality," she said, but then added, "of course, some of the things men say to women are stunningly horrible."

"Form a consciousness-raising group," I said, falling easily, in the presence of a congenial compatriot, into a back-home idiom.

"Oh no, that would never work here. This is not a 'spill your guts' kind of country." She paused, then added, "Though sometimes I think, God knows, they need some kind of reeducation here. Whenever I go to a meeting and speak up, I'm hooted down as a pushy American woman."

As we sat and talked, I noticed she had a lot of afterthoughts, ideas advanced and then qualified. Schools were good, though a bit regimented. Food was always sufficient, but the queues were interminable. She seemed to me to be straddling two worlds, and I asked if she still felt more American than Russian. "This is home. I could never have had the friends I made here. But I'll admit, I am still an 'American,' even to my closest friends. It's partly my material privileges. They envy me my apartment and my trips abroad, but it's more than that. They sense I move at a different rhythm."

The real issue was her son. He went through all of elementary school feeling himself totally Russian. But in high school, when the tyrannical rules of cliques took hold, problems arose. His schoolmates began regarding him as American. By the time he graduated, he was pretty much troubled by the whole thing. He insisted on going to the States for a period, to see what it was like to be the person Russians had assumed he already was.

"Now he's back, but who knows if he intends to stay?" she said.

Later, when I made ready to leave, I asked a final question. "What do you miss most about America, day to day?"

"The peanut butter," she said, and a dreamy look slid across her face, very different from her usual matter-of-fact expression.

As I waited at the bus stop to begin my trip back to city's center, I glanced at Garb's book, which she had given me as we parted. In the epilogue she had written that she lived, "near forests and parks," in a neighborhood with three schools, three child-care centers, a large movie theater, an adult outpatient health center with specialists in all important fields, a similar center for children, a supermarket, several smaller grocery stores, a post office, bank, two beauty salons, two barbershops and abundant greenery. I looked around. Though the items seemed to be in place, they failed utterly to cohere into a "neighborhood." Everything seemed haphazard and unkempt, not so much decaying as never properly conceived in the first place. But, I decided, Garb's words might have served as a description of a neighborhood in an American city, perhaps Denver, somewhat enriched by memory—a place where you ask for peanut butter and the shopkeeper won't screw up his face in astonishment and distaste.

While serving as a secretary to the Russian consul in Philadelphia from 1811 to 1815, Pavel Svinin spent some of his spare time sketching and painting. He left a portfolio of fifty-two watercolors. Many are clichéd views of harbors, public buildings, and picturesque landscapes, but there are also some sharp observations of social life. *Night Life in Philadelphia* is particularly instructive. Beneath a streetlight, a black man is selling oysters off a wagon. He is smiling, but without servility. He and three customers all look attentively toward the focal point of the painting: a young man leaning comfortably against the corner of a building, his face composed in an amiable expression. The people in the picture wear items that mark their class—a tradesman's apron, a woman's commonplace gingham dress, a man's patent leather shoes—but the gathering nevertheless figures a sense of harmony, of pleasures taken in common. In the background is the facade of Chestnut Street Theater, with its classical statuary and formal arcades: it stresses by contrast the easygoing manner animating the action in the foreground. In general, the painting shows an America that is informal, casual, unceremonious, and—most important—benignly sociable as a result.

Though slight as art, Svinin's painting has historical weight. Throughout much of the nineteenth century many Russians echoed the opinion embodied in it; Americans, it was very often said, were capable of refreshingly direct social relations. At their best, Americans had found a way to escape suffocating politesse. Russians' admiration was not altogether surprising, since what they found to like in America was much the same as what they believed prevailed at home, or would, as soon as a few kinks were ironed out.

Social decorum seems a fairly innocuous topic, but Russian judgments about it were never casual; they were wrapped up with the momentous effort to define the country's historical destiny. Russia's intention during much of the nineteenth century was to plot a unique course, a path that would simultaneously avoid the mistakes of other countries and supersede their achievements—the epithet "the Third Rome" had considerable vogue in Russian intellectual circles, and it nicely catches the double aspiration of a surmounting glory and a subverting iconoclasm. But, for all the declarations of having discovered a new way, Russians often wavered and wished for nothing so much as to be just like their European neighbors. The European style proved as hard to resist in matters of social decorum as in theorizing about historical evolution. Though Russians prided themselves on the native capacity for off-the-cuff amiability, they tended to grovel before France's bon ton and the fine manners of the English gentry. America provided Russians with a handy stick to ward off the seductions of Europe. "Personal relations are devoid of empty ceremonies," the chemist Dmitri Mendeleev announced after visiting America in 1890. "Everything that is important becomes established quickly, easily and in direct dealings between individuals. One will never meet that haughtiness which is so characteristic among many in Europe."

But views of the Americans' everyday style had another side. Significantly, Svinin's *Night Life in Philadelphia* stands out among his paintings of America's social life, which typically convey a less enthusiastic judgment. *Members of the City Troop and other Philadelphia Soldiery* shows troops gathered for review. They have a most unmilitary bearing. Two soldiers directly in front of the commander shoulder their rifles nonchalantly and have their arms folded across their chest. Another lolls against a cannon with his legs crossed; he has an expression of amused anticipation, as if waiting for the commander to say something funny. *Merry-making at a Wayside Inn* shows two couples dancing a spirited reel to the accompaniment of a black fiddler. One of the men has not bothered to remove a cigar from his mouth. In the background, in full view but attracting no attention, another well-dressed couple is kissing. The passengers in *Travel by Stage Coach near Trenton* include a woman whose skirt is billowing in the breeze, a man with his arm slung over his seatback and his leg propped up against the sideboard, another man with his handkerchief out, having just finished or being just about to blow his nose. All too often, it appears, our conviviality slips over toward the indecorous, our admirably informal style becomes slightly too unbuttoned.

Svinin drew a fine line between the attractive and the repellent, and there was in general a remarkable fluidity to Russian judgments of our social behavior. When we were good, we were very good, but as often we were horrid. If we were an example of how to avoid Europe's stuffy style, we were also a warning of what happened when informality went too far. Alexander Lakier, the author of *Journey through the North American States, Canada and Cuba,* noted with approval the absence in the United States Congress of the pomp that marked the English Parliament. ". . . here [in America]," he notes, "there are neither wigs nor formal dress nor decorations. Everyone wears a black frockcoat and sits where he pleases." But then, hardly missing a beat, Lakier adds, "Had I not felt regret for the nice new furniture and carpet in the House of Representatives, I would not even have noticed the rude, but perhaps comfortable position of the feet raised by a son of the plains above the head of his neighbor, and the nasty habit many Americans have of chewing tobacco. . . ." In the space of two sentences, admiration turns to disdain, warm affection to distaste.

In *The Possessed,* Dostoevsky offered his own comment on American manners. Recalling his trip through America a character remarks, "One day when we were traveling, a chap put his hand into my pocket, took out my hairbrush, and began brushing his hair with it. [We] just glanced at each other and made up our minds that it was quite all right and that we liked it very much." This cameo is purely a product of Dostoevsky's perfervid imagination (he never visited America), and it is doubtful that many readers believed filching hairbrushes from strangers was common American practice; but Dostoevsky had succeeded in underscoring an important feature of Russian opinion. In making the act of taking the hairbrush appear absolutely casual and without malice, Dostoevsky shows American behavior as thoroughly impulsive, ad hoc. Americans made up the rules as they went along.

It followed, indeed, that Americans could as easily sin on the side of bizarre pretentiousness as of crudeness. To visiting Russians, America was a place where every encounter might turn equally into a scandal or a punctilious bore. "Then began an endlessly long dinner with vast pretensions," Tchaikovsky remarked with disgust of an evening in New York high society. "For instance everyone was served ice cream in the form of an enormous life-like rose." Let it stand, that rose—a symbol of nineteenth-century Russian opinion that Americans' social behavior always threatened to slip away from a norm of dignified moderation.

The Bolshevik Revolution should have brought change—good manners are presumably not a major concern of proletarians building a new world. But to a remarkable degree Russians continued to worry about American behavior. The judgment remained more or less the same. Though American informality was sometimes praised, we were most often scorned for our immoderation. The Soviet counterpart of Pavel Svinin was Alexander Deyneka, who was one of the few Russian painters to visit America (in 1935) until *glasnost* opened the doors, and it is to the point that Deyneka produced nothing comparable to Svinin's *Night Life in Philadelphia*. His attitude is best represented by two drawings, which taken together form a telling diptych. *American Women* shows three fashionably dressed women strolling on a boulevard. High-heeled, in long dresses and with small, military-looking caps, they project a forbidding formality. Their expressions are cold and haughty, and there is no suggestion of communication—though one woman has her head turned to another, her pose implies an elegant posturing, not an eagerness to talk. *Vaudeville Dance* also depicts three women, but makes a diametrically different point. The women wear short costumes, revealing an aggressive physicality. Their flexed, heavily muscled legs and hunched shoulders lack all delicacy. Only one of the women's faces is distinct; the eyes are closed and the mouth twisted into a simulacrum of passion. Taken together the paintings argue that Americans oscillate between two extremes—bizarrely crude or showily pretentious.

It is tempting to dismiss postrevolutionary criticism of American manners as merely ideology by another name. Capitalism, goes the argument, corrupts human as well as economic relations, forcing men and women into grotesque attitudes. If Lenin had it right, Americans were not merely boors as well as exploiters, but boors because exploiters. The ideological argument can be persuasive, but it is doubtful that it plays a central role. There is an edgy distaste in Russian opinion that points to something visceral. "Americans are by nature a chewing people," Ilf and Petrov reported. "They chew gum, candy, the ends of cigars; their jaws are always moving, clicking and snapping." Such comment seems beyond politics; it is disdain pure and simple. "Often in the cafeteria," Mayakovsky noted grimly, "food is given without awaiting the patron's order— it is just what he always takes." (Ilf and Petrov claimed that Americans filled up on food "just as an automobile fills up on gas.") Since eating is only ingestion, it follows that our cuisine must be contemptible, and that is how Russians have always treated it. From Boris Pilnyak's remark in 1931 that the " 'hot dog' was, given its taste, appropriately named," down to the comments in current newspapers, Russians seem hardly able to suppress their disgust. ("American food is somehow unfit for human beings, somehow artificial," I read in *Nedelya*.) It is less likely that our manners provide an excuse for ideological condemnation than the reverse— Marxism provides the terms to express a deeply felt distaste for our forms of behavior.

Sergei Eisenstein's experience in Hollywood in 1935 (he had

come at Paramount's invitation) provides a focal point in the history of Russian complaints about how we live. Eisenstein endured a string of disappointments in America. Paramount rejected his idea for a film about the California gold rush on the grounds that American audiences did not want to see their country's history retold by a foreigner; his hopes for a film based on Dreiser's *An American Tragedy* were dashed by back-stabbing studio politics; and finally he lost his contract when the studio caved in to pressure from a congressional committee chaired by the Red-baiting Hamilton Fish. It is not surprising that Eisenstein's description of the Hollywood film crowd emphasized the deceit and sham of its behavior. "They all drank hard, ran around in wonderful automobiles, breaking all the traffic rules and speed limits when the policemen weren't looking, buying them off when they did." But it is his conclusion that should bring us up short. "They got tanned, smearing themselves with thick layers of cream against sunburn, and went in for ocean bathing." Americans, it seems, are not only hypocritical but innately vulgar. We violate rules of decency even when we think we are behaving normally.

I try to watch my step in Russia. Nevertheless some little thing always throws me. I have navigated through far-ranging discussions about the meaning of life without giving offense and have found common ground with fire-breathing ideologues, but I invariably violate one trivial social convention or another. When I forget to leave my coat in the checkroom and instead drape it over the back of my chair, waitresses lecture me on good manners as if I were a child. Or I find that I have somehow offended a caller when I inform him he's dialed the wrong number. "So I have the wrong number, do I!" he bellows as if his honor had been called into question. Tripping over the codes of decorum is disorienting—strolling through the day, you suddenly fall into a black hole of misunderstanding.

On this last trip I had a running dispute with the maid who cleaned my hotel room. The towels that were provided were ridiculously inadequate, no more than dishrags really, making of every shower a tedious, hour-long process. I asked the maid for something that absorbed water instead of moving it around from one part of my body to another. She told me there was nothing she could do.

Later, I bribed a porter with a pack of Marlboros, and he returned with two towels hidden under his jacket. It turned out they were exactly like the ones hanging limply in my bathroom only somewhat larger; a bit better for show, but they wouldn't dry a person any quicker.

The next time the maid cleaned my room she noticed the new towels. "It's not right," she told me. "Those towels are for the deluxe room. You did not pay for deluxe."

"It's just a towel," I said.

"Here in Russia," she said pointedly, "you get what you are entitled to, no more, no less." The Revolution did not change that.

Indeed, if the towels didn't do the job towels were supposed to do, they served very nicely to establish an etiquette. Even if the only means they have at their disposal is patching together tiny pieces of cloth into a slightly larger piece of cloth, Russians will mark the lines of proper behavior.

Sports have provided Russians with some of their most conclusive proof of Americans' intemperate behavior. The rest of the world has noticed that American athletes act like bad-tempered children, but the Soviets have elevated this to an incontrovertible truth. Athletic contests between our two countries have often served them as case studies in good manners (theirs) and bad (ours). When we cackle and prance in victory or whine in defeat, Russians nod knowingly and file the image in the bulging file of our improprieties.

When their national hockey team toured America for the first time, our players resorted to bully-boy tactics, forgetting the puck entirely in their eagerness to shove and to hit; the Soviets responded with some elegant skating and passing, proving not only superior talent but better taste. In tennis matches, when their American opponents scream and quarrel with the referee, the Soviet players wait with detached curiosity for the tantrum to blow over. The most memorable moment in this sorry history was in the 1972 Olympics, when the Soviet basketball team defeated the much-favored Americans. The game ended in a dispute over the referee's decision, and the next day the American team refused to attend the medal ceremony, instead continuing to protest. "When we learned that the Americans had lodged a protest," recalled coach Sergei Bashkin, "we went over to them and asked, 'What's the matter? Why the protest? You know yourselves everything was correct. Why are you tormenting our boys and your own?' " The tone of aggrieved sportsmanship is a bit overdone, but the point has been made: more than mastering the jump shot, Americans should learn to mind their manners.

The official line is that sports are a mirror of morality. In America, the argument goes, the rage to win at all costs reflects the survival-of-the-fittest mentality that contaminates all bourgeois activity. In Russia, sports are an aspect of a harmonious society. In the period immediately after the Revolution, indeed, there was briefly an effort made to invent noncompetitive "socialist" sports. That project didn't get very far, but a related idea—that athletic victory depended on the same qualities as those required of a good citizen—did take hold in the Russian imagination. Americans compete to win; but Russians purportedly compete for the pleasure of it, though (luckily for them) their zest for good, clean fun often brings victory as a sort of side effect. However you define it, the difference in the way we approach sports is considerable.

Going for a walk one day in the Lenin Hills, I noticed a pickup basketball game in progress, and I stopped to watch. The participants ranged in age from late adolescence to early twenties; a couple of them looked a bit winded, but most were in shape, and they ran up and down the court at a good pace. It was a lively game, but something was missing. It took me a minute to realize what it was. There was an absence of exultation. There was no crowing

in triumph, no boisterous shouting. Everyone played earnestly—
no high-fives, no behind-the-back dribbling. I don't mean to say
the players weren't enjoying themselves, or that there wasn't any
spirit to the game. There was. But it was not basketball as I knew
it. It seemed like an old silent black-and-white film that I was used
to seeing in bright primary colors and with a jazzy score.

Then, as I was about to walk away, one of the players executed
a neat reverse lay-up. Jogging back down the court, he turned in
my direction, smiled, and punched the air in the American gesture
of self-congratulation. He obviously had picked out my nationality,
for he also added an exuberant "Okay!" for my benefit.

I found myself smiling as I walked back to the metro station,
cheered by the encounter. It had been trivial, of course, but in a
history of gaffes and blunders and misunderstandings, every spark
of connection deserves to be honored. The young man had paid us
the homage of imitation, yet he had kept his gesture just enough
off-center to preserve a self-defining irony—which, now that I
thought about it, might serve nicely as a model for how Russians
and Americans should behave whenever they meet.

# Afterword

During most of my trip to Russia, up until the last days, I was dismayed by the passivity which most Russians seemed to show in the face of history. Even as they live through the freedom of the age of Gorbachev, the old attitudes about America shackle them. Go and make a new future, I often wanted to exclaim, free of old stereotypes and dried-out received wisdom. But something happened—something personal—that made me review these brave words. I was persuaded that it is not so easy to get around history.

The history in my case was family history. My father was born in Grodno. The city occasionally passed to Poland's control, but Russian was my father's first language and he attended Russian schools. He left Grodno in 1920, lived in Germany for a few years, then moved on to Paris in 1929, where he met my mother. He had an independent streak that helped him elude the embrace of my mother's family, but it was at best a stalemate. The Kahans were hard to resist. They were numerous, and their history had the sweep of at least a mini-epic, spanning centuries and continents and marked by fortunes made and lost. It is this story that I think of when I think of my Russian past.

The Kahans were not Russians but Jews living in Russia, which was something quite different. At the beginning of the nineteenth century, my great-great-grandfather had a lumber business in a town some ninety miles southwest of Minsk. The logs were floated to market along the Berezina River, a tributary of the Dnieper. The business prospered. With some of his profit, my great-great-grandfather purchased Lyalichi, a palace that once belonged to Catherine the Great. He immediately proceeded to dismantle it and sell off the elegant carvings, gold faucets, and brass doorknobs. When my grandmother told this story, she said it showed a lack of culture. But I found it amusing and a bit inspiring. Russia kept my family and other Jews at the edge of society, confining them to the Pale of Settlement and restricting them to certain occupations. Russia made my family merchants—very well, we would merchandise its cultural treasures. My interpretation figured to be different from my grandmother's. For her the story was a living part of her tumultuous Russian existence; I viewed it with the curiosity of a noncombatant.

The focus of the family's history was Azerbaijan. My great-grandfather Chaim Kahan had a thriving kerosene business in Brest-Litovsk, but when he realized that oil was the fuel of the future he moved the family to Baku, near the oil fields. The Russian oil industry at the turn of this century was dominated by the giant companies Nobel of Sweden and DeBeers of South Africa, and later the Rothschilds; but during its beginnings, anyway, there were openings for the little man. Chaim Kahan squeezed through, in one case by taking advantage of what would now be called a tax loophole. The business was speculative, and there were periodic losses, but my great-grandfather apparently had the risk-taking mentality required to make a go of it. At its high point, the family business owned a couple of tankers and had branch offices in Denmark and Germany, as well as running Baku's Yiddish-language newspaper on the side.

The family lived in style, though far from the Croesus level of the high tsarist aristocracy. They occupied an elegant apartment on Nicolaevsky Street, across from a park. My grandfather went to the English Club every evening to play cards. My grandmother occupied herself with volunteer community work and running a household with seven servants. There were vacations on the Baltic coast. There was also an apartment and office in Petersburg—in recognition of his service to the oil industry, Chaim Kahan was made a *kupets pervoy gildii* (merchant of the first guild) which allowed him and his family to live anywhere in the empire instead of being confined to the Pale.

The Revolution abruptly destroyed this way of life, and many of those who were forced out of Russia in those years never got over their material losses. They spent their time concocting plots to reclaim their patrimony, and were ready to pick up and return to Russia as soon as word came that the Bolshevik regime was faltering. This nostalgic longing was so common in émigré circles that there was a phrase for it: *sidet na chimodanakh* (to sit on one's suitcases). But the Kahans seemed hardly to have looked back. In none of the stories that came down to me was there a note of regret. When my mother first came to America she worked in a chocolate factory to help make ends meet, a far cry from the life she would have had in Baku. The smell of raw cocoa still nauseates her; but whiffs of imperial Russia that have come her way over the years have left her unmoved.

The 1917 Revolution was of course about politics as well as ownership, but family stories touched on this theme only obliquely. That makes sense. Though it was a time of ideological passion, the Kahans occupied uncertain ground between the contending camps. As bourgeoisie, they were targets for the Reds; one of my uncles was on a hit list, and made his escape, disguised as a peasant, in the nick of time. But the Whites were hardly more congenial, since many of them were lethally anti-Semitic. (Whites knifed to death one of my maternal grandmother's sisters and her family in their Kharkov home, just for the sport of it.) By this standard, the Red Army with its commander-in-chief Leon Trotsky (originally, Leon Bronstein) did not seem so bad. At a remove of time and space, the Revolution could seem a clear-cut conflict; up close, the lines of allegiance were fuzzy.

One of my favorite stories is about my Uncle Lolya. In 1919, when he was sixteen the family had taken temporary refuge in Kharkov. It was during one of the interludes when that city was occupied by the Whites, and he decided more or less as a lark to join up. He dressed up in a makeshift White Army uniform and was put to standing sentry. When she heard of this, the family nanny, a peasant woman given to direct action, marched down to his post and dragged him home, disregarding his loud protests. It's hard to sort out the elements of allegiance, whim, and the pull of daily life that this episode contains. Certainly, there is little in the way of lessons that might be relevant for life in America. But as a story it's just fine.

When I was in Leningrad once I decided to go and have a look at the old family home on Stremyannaya Street. My idea of it depended entirely on certain disjointed facts relayed by an elderly uncle. The bottom floor, he had told me, served as the family's business office, and the men of the family would repair there after breakfast, wearing their formal cutaways. In the large anteroom there hung a portrait of the tsar—the law required it, my uncle said with an apologetic shrug. The city's most popular bathhouse stood at the end of the street. During a political demonstration in the hectic days before the Revolution, a mob on its way to topple the statue of a tsarist general on a nearby square suddenly began stoning all the houses on Stremyannaya Street. Those were all the facts I got, since my uncle's memory was fading fast.

No. 19 Stremyannaya Street proved to be a nondescript four-story building with a narrow driveway leading into a courtyard. Off the driveway was a double door, through which I entered. There was an acrid odor in the entryway, typical for those older houses in Leningrad where the battle against garbage and dirt has tailed off into something like a stalemate. I went up one flight of stairs, to what must have been the family residence, and rang the bell. No one answered. Looking at the blank door, I felt stymied. I stood on the landing for another minute and then left. Outside again, I asked a passerby to take a snapshot of me with Stremyannaya Street as background. If it had been possible, the force of my desire would have made my camera capable of spectral photography, and the ghosts of my ancestors, in their black cutaways, would have appeared when the print was developed—proof positive that the past responds when called. But of course I knew that all I would really get would be Stremyannaya Street *circa* 1985, with the bathhouse at the corner which, I had been told, was still one of the most popular in town. The past had not vanished—all the facts were stored away in my mind—but it did seem inert and unresponsive, a layabout not capable of a hard day's work.

On my last visit to Russia, I didn't go to any old family sites, but I did arrange to meet a man who had known the Kahans in Baku. A year before my trip my mother had finally returned to the Soviet Union after staying away for almost seven decades; on a whim, she had tried to get in touch with Boris Fridman, who had lived next door to the Kahans on Nicolaevsky Street, and against all odds she had succeeded. The Fridmans had been wealthy, fabulously so, but despite his family's haut bourgeois status Boris Fridman had decided not to emigrate at the time of the Revolution. He stayed on and made a good career for himself as a cinematographer.

How did a Jew from a wealthy bourgeois background manage to get ahead during those years? When my mother met him in Moscow, he was reticent about his past. In general he held himself aloof. My mother showed me a snapshot someone took to commemorate her visit; Fridman stands a few feet apart from the group, as if trying to insinuate that he really didn't know these people. But when my mother told him I would be coming to Moscow the following year he warmed up briefly. He asked if it would be possible for me to bring him a portable tape recorder. He needed it for his work.

I called Fridman when I was already packing to depart. He invited me to lunch at the restaurant in Dom Kino in whose film school he taught. He was already there when I arrived, seated at a centrally located table with his wife. After saying hello, he lost interest in me immediately. He concentrated on acknowledging greetings from students and colleagues, and occasionally whispering a bit of school gossip to his wife. She spoke to me exclusively about Fridman's diet, enumerating the foods he had eaten for the last week; he corrected her once or twice. About my life in America, he asked not one question. It was a dreary meal. It was only when dessert was on the table that he addressed me directly. "The Kahans," he said, just as if we had been discussing the topic for hours, "I would say they were a well-off family, though they tried to give the appearance of belonging to the upper class."

The meanness of the remark took me by surprise. I suppose, thinking back, that he was only trying to cheer himself up. It was probably distressing having to rely on the son of a childhood friend for such a simple thing as a tape recorder, and he may have wanted to spell out the terms of the transaction. I was wealthier than the Kahans by far, he was saying, but I remained in Russia to make a good life and career, as you can see just by looking around.

At the time, however, I was too annoyed for analysis. I was provoked, roused. My Russian past, which often had seemed contingent and lacking heft, snapped into vivid shape. Fridman had gotten it wrong from top to bottom, from the Kahans' social circumstances to their attitudes toward emigration, and I could not let that pass. A sequence of events that had been lying dormant now seemed alive. No longer just a story told in New York City apartments, it was part of a living argument.

I decided a rebuttal was in order, and as we walked back to the anteroom to collect our coats I reviewed the options. I could simply not mention the tape recorder, leaving Fridman to assume his request had been ignored. But that seemed excessive punishment. Or I could hand the tape recorder over while adding an ungracious comment. But anything I said would go right by him, leaving him in smug possession of what he wanted. It seemed to come down to yes or no, with nothing in between: this last event that I was adding to the skein constituting my family's hisory in Russia would be either pure meanness or pure kindness, both of which seemed equally unfitting. In the end, I presented him with the package.

He took it with excitement, walking over to a corner where he could open it without attracting the attention of passersby. He removed the wrapping excitedly. Then, suddenly, his face fell in disappointment. It was, he explained to me, a mini-recorder. The Soviet Union had not begun even to think of producing such models or, more to the point, the batteries to run them.

I returned to my hotel, pleased despite myself with how it had worked out. Fridman had gotten his tape recorder and would be able to use it until the batteries that had been included ran down— some ten hours of satisfaction was more or less what he deserved, I reckoned. It had been sheer luck, of course, but I felt I had found just the right gesture to deal with the past.

It didn't take me long to realize how fatuous I had been. Fridman's relation with my family was a long and complicated one— years of visiting every day in Baku, playing cards, running through attics, having stupid arguments and cheery reconciliations. It was a history made up of subtle changes of emotion. It didn't make sense to try to confront it with a showy gesture involving hard-to-get batteries—or to put it another way, if you are going to think about the past at all, you must honor it, acknowledge every scintilla of its meanings. It's not enough to think up little tricks that will get you past the awkward moments.

Many of the Russians I had met on my trip had also not had an easy time trying to find a way to deal with history. Now that America stands before them as a living fact instead of a dim idea, they have to come to terms with it. I had once thought this coming to terms could be done by just a bit of daring or bravado, but I see it is more complicated than that.

But if it is hard to see immediate success, it is still not necessary to be excessively pessimistic. Though the common history of our two countries has imposed a pattern we must follow, it has not shackled us with an iron logic. We cannot escape the past, cannot jump into new more auspicious circumstance; but we can move forward inch by inch, I thought, and kept the idea in mind as I packed, rode out to the airport, boarded, and headed homeward.

# Bibliographical Note

The research of others has helped me. I have listed below those books that either pointed me toward little-known facts or offered unusual interpretations. But where I have used material that was generally available, I have not given a particular source.

*General Histories*
    N. N. Bolkhovitinov, *Stanovlenie russko-amerikanskikh otnoshenii (The Beginnings of Russian-American Relations)*. Moscow, 1965.
    G. P. Kuropyatnik, *Rossiya i SShA (Russia and the United States)*. Moscow, 1981.
    N. V. Sivachev and N. N. Yakovlev, *Russia and the United States*. Chicago: University of Chicago Press, 1979.

*Economics*
    Kendall E. Bailes, *Technology and Society Under Lenin and Stalin*. Princeton, New Jersey: Princeton University Press, 1978.
    Allan Nevins and Frank Hill, *Ford: Expansionism and Challenge*. New York: Scribner, 1957.
    N. N. Smelyakov, *Delovaya America (Business America)*. Moscow, 1969.

Charles Sorensen, *My Forty Years with Ford*. New York: Norton, 1956.

V. S. Virginskii, *Robert Fulton*. Moscow, 1965/ Washington, 1976.

*Americans in Russia*

Allison Blakely, *Russia and the Negro*. Washington, D.C.: Howard University Press, 1986.

David Caute, *Fellow Travellers*. New York: Macmillan, 1973.

Martin B. Duberman, *Paul Robeson*. New York: Knopf, 1989.

Ruth Epperson Kennell, *Theodore Dreiser and the Soviet Union 1927– 1945*. New York: International Publishers, 1969.

Sylvia R. Margulies, *Pilgrimage to Russia . . . [1924–1937]*. Madison, Wisconsin: University of Wisconsin Press, 1968.

Samuel Eliot Morison, *John Paul Jones*. Boston: Atlantic Monthly Press, 1959.

J. P. Morray, *Project Kuzbas: American Workers in Siberia [1921–1926]*. New York: International Publishers, 1983.

G. Ya. Tarle, *Druzya strany Sovetov (Friends of the Country of the Soviets)*. Moscow, 1968.

Stephan Watrous, ed., *John Ledyard's Journey Through Russia and Siberia [1787–1788]*. Madison, Wisconsin: University of Wisconsin Press, 1966.

*Russians in America*

James R. Gibson, ed., *Imperial Russia in Frontier America*. New York: Oxford University Press, 1976.

Ivor Montagu, *With Eisenstein in Hollywood*. New York: International Publishers, 1969.

Avrahm Yarmolinsky, *A Russian's American Dream*. Lawrence, Kansas: University of Kansas Press, 1965.

Elkhonon Yoffe, *Tchaikovsky in America*. New York: Oxford University Press, 1986.

*Cultural Relations*

K. A. Ashin and A. P. Miller, *V tiskakh dukhovnogo gneta (In the Vise of Spiritual Decay)*. Moscow, 1986.

Jeffrey Brooks, *When Russia Learned to Read*. Princeton, New Jersey: Princeton University Press, 1985.

# Bibliographical Note

Kornei Chukovsky, *Kniga o sovremennykh pisatelyakh (A Book About Contemporary Writers)*. St. Petersburg, 1914.

Gordon McVay, *Isadora & Esenin*. Ann Arbor, Michigan: Ardis, 1980.

Raisa Orlova, *Kheminguey v Rossii (Hemingway in Russia)*. Ann Arbor, Michigan: Ardis, 1985.

S. Frederick Starr: *Red and Hot: The Fate of Jazz in the Soviet Union [1917–1980]*. New York: Oxford University Press, 1980. Also: "OAS: The Union of Contemporary Architects," in *Russian Modernism,* ed., George Gibian and H. W. Tjalsma. Ithaca, New York: Cornell University Press, 1976.

Richard Taylor, *The Politics of the Soviet Cinema.* Cambridge, Massachusetts, 1979.

O. E. Tuganova, *Vzaimodeystvie kultur SSSR i SShA (Cultural Interactions of the U.S.S.R. and U.S.A.),* 1987.

Robert C. Williams, *Russian Art and American Money.* Cambridge, Massachusetts: Harvard University Press, 1980.

My thanks to Allan Pollard of Firestone Library, Princeton University.

*211*

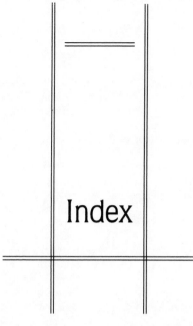

# Index

Academy of Sciences, Soviet, 64
Adams, John Quincy, 25–26
affection, 31, 35, 36, 37, 96,
    100–103
  idealization as basis of, 11, 19
*Airport* (Hailey), 162
Aksyonov, Vasily, 109, 131,
    132, 155
*Alba Madonna* (Raphael), 146
Alcoholics Anonymous, 109–14,
    115, 116
Aldridge, Ira, 184
Alexei, Tsar, 114, 115
Ali, Muhammad, 97
Allied Expeditionary Force
    (1918), 23, 97–98
Alvin Ailey dance company, 167
ambivalence, 10–12, 17–20, 90,
    134
  American heroes and, 96–100
  about American methods, 60,
    65–66, 92
  coping with, 93–95
  in jokes, 105

visiting foreigners and, 183–
    191
  *see also* affection; hostility
*America: A Heart to Heart Conver-
    sation*, 126–27
America as model, *see* model,
    America as
American Agency for Cultural
    Ties with the Soviet Union,
    139
"American Circle," at Kiev Uni-
    versity, 38
"American City, The" (Magni-
    togorsk), 185, 186
American Communist party, 34,
    65
American national character, 16,
    86–116, 135
  admired traits in, 96–100,
    191–92
  competitiveness in, 197–98
  Cowboys in, 90–91
  demystification of, 119–25,
    136

American national character
(*cont.*)
pragmatism in, 90–95
Russian exploitation of, 105–7
Russian national character vs.,
107–16, 181
Russians as "experts" on, 11,
86, 103–4, 162
*see also* images of America;
model, America as
American Philosophical Society
of Philadelphia, 27–28
*American Tragedy, An* (Dreiser),
196
*American Women*, 194–95
AMO auto parts factory, 64
Anzhaparidze, Georgi, 161–65
Appleton, Nathan, 184
*Appointment with California* (Kon-
drashev), 132
Arbat, 160, 164
Arbatov, Georgi, 67–68
architecture, 133–38
Aronson, Boris, 147
art:
Bolshevik Revolution and,
145–46
high vs. low, 165–68
new categories of, 168, 171
*see also* cultural treasures,
Russian
artists, émigré, 144–45, 149, 152,
153
Artyomev, Vyacheslav, 165
Association of Contemporary
Architects, 135
Astro Pizza, 14
Auer, Mischa, 147

Bardin, T. S., 64
Baseball Hall of Fame, 11
Bashkin, Sergei, 198

basketball, 198–99
*Battleship Potemkin*, 172
behavior, proper, 28–29, 31,
107–15, 181–82, 191–99
European vs. American, 192,
193
Russian vs. American, 92,
193–98
World War II and, 29
Benjamin, Walter, 129
Berdan, Hiram, 73, 95
Berdanka rifle, 73
Beryozka stores, 187
*Biloxi Blues*, 13
Black Hundreds, The, 183
Blok, Alexander, 18, 134
Bolkhovitinov, N. N., 25–26
*Bolshaya Entsiklopediya*, 62
bookstores, Soviet, 154–57, 160
American-managed, 155–57
boorishness, as American fault,
194, 195, 196
braggart, as American type, 97
Brodsky, Joseph, 87
Budapest String Quartet, 148
Bukharin, Nikolai, 99
Burnett, Carol, 107, 109
*Business America (Delovaya Amer-
ika)* (Smelyakov), 120

Café Pirosmani, 96
Caldwell, Erskine, 26
California, 132
canniness, as American trait, 97
Carter, Joe, 44–46
cartoons, 42, 44, 77
Catherine the Great, 27, 80, 88,
89, 105–6, 201
Catholicism, 114
Cedarvale, Kans., 38, 39
celebrities, 26, 172–73, 184
censorship, 157–60

# Index

Central Labor Institute, 63
Chaikovsky, Nikolai, 38
Chaplin, Charlie, 102, 166
Cheever, John, 159
Chernyshevsky, Nikolai, 38
Chicago, Ill., 132
Chopadaev, N.C., 154
Chukovsky, Kornei, 160
Churchill, Sir Winston, 29, 33
cities:
    Soviet vs. American, 128–38
    as symbols, 129–33
citizen exchanges, 180
civil rights movement, American, 43
Civil War, American, 28–29
Civil War, Spanish, 157
Cliburn, Van, 26, 166
"Cloud Project" (Lissitzky), 135
Colt, Samuel, 183
commissar mentality, 85
*Communist, The*, 38
condescension, 24–26, 143–44
confessional style, 107–14
Conover, Willis, 141
consumer goods, American:
    mystique of, 74–76, 81–83
    quality of, 74, 77
utility of, 73
consumerism, 76–83
    Soviet acceptance of, 76–77
*Contradictory America
    (Protivorechivaya Amerika)*, 125
Cooper, Hugh, 184
Cooper, James Fenimore, 11
Coppola, Francis Ford, 168
Corbett, Harvey Wiley, 137
Cowboys, in American national
    character, 90–91
*Crime and Punishment* (Dostoevsky), 116
CRT arbitage firm, 68, 70, 72

cuisine, American, 195
cultural exchanges, 15, 27
    American artistic skills in, 139–
        143, 148–52, 166–68, 172–76
    antagonistic views in, 143–44
    difficulties in, 140
    preconceptions and, 141, 143,
        176–77
    time lapses in, 159–61
    *see also* people-to-people di-
        plomacy
cultural treasures, Russian:
    loss of, 144–48, 164
    pride in, 153–54
curiosity, 108–9
currency regulations, 118

Dashkova, Princess, 28
Davies, Joseph E., 146
Davis, Bette, 172
DeBeers oil company, 201
Decembrist Uprising, 55, 56
Dell, Floyd, 26
demystification, 119–24, 125,
    136
Detgiz Publishers, 158
Detroit, Mich., 132–33
*D. E. Trust, The*, 76
Deyneka, Alexander, 194–95
Dialog, 68–71
differences between America and
    Russia, 92, 94–95, 108, 116
diplomatic relations, 23–24, 25–
    26, 62
Disney, Roy, 173, 174–75, 176
Disney, Walt, 173–76
    Marshak vs., 176
Dom Kino, 58, 153
Dom Knigi (House of Books),
    137, 138
Dom Mody (House of Fashion),
    73–74

# Index

*Donald Duck's Crime*, 175
Dos Passos, John, 26, 155
Dostoevsky, F. M., 116, 193–94
*Downbeat*, 128
Dreiser, Theodore, 26, 74–75, 99, 196
drugstores, American, 121
Duncan, Isadora, 137–38, 179–181
Dylan, Bob, 160

Eastern Orthodox religion, 114
Edison, Thomas, 97
efficiency, 50–54, 92, 94
  capitalism as model for, 63
  convenience and, 51–53
  decline of, 66
Ehrenburg, Ilya, 76
Eisenhower, Dwight D., 32
Eisenstein, Sergei, 74, 135–36, 153, 172, 173, 195–96
Ellington, Duke, 140, 141, 142, 143, 167
*Emperor of Russia, The*, 52
Empire State Building, 135
Ermolaev Theater, 148, 149
Esenin, Sergei, 118, 131, 138, 179–81
etiquette, *see* behavior, proper
Evetushenko, Evgeny, 126
Executive Board of Moscow region, 55
*Extraordinary Adventures of Mr. West in the Land of the Bolsheviks, The*, 100–101

Fairbanks, Douglas, 172
famine relief program (1921), 26
*Fantasia*, 175
fashion, 72–74, 78, 82
Faulkner, William, 162
favors and gifts, American, 10, 20, 81, 83, 204

Ferriss, Hugh, 137
films:
  American, 72, 124, 166, 172–176
  Soviet, 58–61, 100–101, 124, 153
Finland, 86
Fish, Hamilton, 196
Flanagan, Thomas, 162
Fokine, Valery, 149–52
Fonda, Henry, 172
food service, 53–54, 56–57
Ford, Henry, 19, 61, 62–63, 66, 96
Ford, 61–62, 64
foreigners, *see* visitors, American
*Forest Fire*, 144
*For Whom the Bell Tolls* (Hemingway), 156, 157, 159
Fox, Gustavus, 29, 103
Franklin, Benjamin, 26–28, 90, 96
Freeman, Joseph, 26
Fridman, Boris, 204–6
Frost, Robert, 87
Fulton, Robert, 51–52
fur traders, Russian, 19

Garb, Paula, 188–91
Garfield, John, 102
Gastev, Alexander, 63
Gaz-A car, 61
Geins, Vladimir, 38–40
General Electric, 62, 183
*General Line, The*, 75, 153
genius, 26, 165–68, 173
gift giving, *see* favors and gifts, American
Gogol, N. V., 130
*Golden Calf, The* (Ilf and Petrov), 124
*Gone With the Wind* (Mitchell), 162

Gorbachev, Raisa, 110
Gorky, Maksim, 75, 99, 163
Gorky Affair, 99
Gorky Park, 15–16, 168
Goryachev, Sergei, 55–57
Grey, Zane, 90
group behavior, 46–47

Hailey, Arthur, 167
Hammer, Armand, 146
Hammett, Dashiell, 163
Harding, Warren, 26
Hard Rock Café, 168–69
Haywood, William ("Big Bill"),
    66
Heifetz, Jascha, 147
Heller, Joseph, 163
Hemingway, Ernest, 97, 156,
    157, 158–60, 162
Hermitage (Leningrad), 146
heroes:
    Americans as, 26–28, 62–63,
    96–100, 105, 107, 174
    ideology and, 98–99
    political leaders as, 98
    reticence and, 97
Hero of Our Time, A (Lermon-
    tov), 141–42
Herzen, Alexander, 17, 89
history:
    continuing impact of, 206–7
    preconceptions and, 200
hockey, 197
Hollywood, 196
    as model, 59
    stars in, 172
Horowitz, Vladimir, 147, 148
hostility, 10, 18, 85–86, 118
Hotel Intourist, 54
Hotel Metropol, 166
Hotel National, 14, 153, 173
Hotel Rossiya, 13–14, 139, 140,
    141

Houston, Whitney, 77
Huckleberry Finn (Twain), 17
Hudson Navigational Company,
    51–52
Hughes, Langston, 43
humor, see cartoons; jokes

ideology:
    American heroes and, 98–
    99
    architecture and, 133–38
    assembly-line methods and,
    63
    of class struggle, 76
    consumerism and, 76–77
    Disney cartoons and, 173, 176
    joint ventures and, 61–62
    literature and, 155, 156–60,
    161, 163
    Marxist philosophy vs. theory
    in, 115
    social decorum and, 195, 198
    social efficiency and, 54–58
    social organization and, 46–47
    stereotyping and, 13
    suspicions about, 119
Ilf, Ilya, 19, 52, 120–24, 125,
    126, 132, 195
illegal transactions, 20, 21
images of America, 15, 16–20,
    86–95, 130–33
    exemplary American in, 86
    idealization in, 19, 26–27, 62,
    87, 98–100
    as image of Russia, 19
    recent changes in, 124–28
    typical sought in, 130
    as uninformed, 15, 89
    see also American national
    character
industrial design, 78–81
Industrial Designers of America,
    77–81

# Index

Industrial Workers of the World, 66

inferiority complex, 23–24

information:
  about American daily life, 72–73
  scarcity of, 11, 15, 86
  television as source of, 124–125, 127

*Innocents Abroad, The* (Twain), 26

*Inostrannaya literatura (Foreign Literature)*, 158

insensitivity, 30–31

Institute of United States and Canada, 67, 95

International Communications Agency, 158

International Harvester Co., 62

*International Herald Tribune*, 158

Intourist, 87

*Invitation to an Execution* (Nabokov), 149–51

*It's a Mad, Mad, Mad, Mad World*, 166

Ives, Charles, 167

*Izvestia*, 77, 132

Jackson, Michael, 82

jazz, 10, 43, 128, 141, 142, 166

Jefferson, Thomas, 88

Jews, Soviet, 201, 202, 204

joint ventures, Soviet-American, 26, 28, 55–56, 67, 183, 184
  in automobile production, 61–63
  in book publishing, 161
  business techniques in, 69
  in computer software, 68–72
  in filmmaking, 58
  in restaurant business, 56–57

jokes:
  about America, 25, 103–4, 186
  about Soviet Union, 53, 67, 77

Jones, John Paul, 105–7

Jones, Quincy, 169

*Joseph Accused by Potiphar's Wife* (Rembrandt), 146

*Journey Through the North American States, Canada and Cuba* (Lakier), 52, 94, 193

Kahan, Chaim, 201–2

Kahan, Lolya, 203

Kahan family, 200–206

Kahn, Albert, 61

Kamskiy Automobile Factory, 69

Kataev, Valentin, 130, 186

Keaton, Buster, 172

Kennan, George, 31, 103

Kennedy, John F., 98

Kent, Rockwell, 153, 168

Khrushchev, Nikita, 119, 170

Khudozhestvennaya literatura, 161–62

Kiev University, 38

*King Kong*, 13

*Kiss of Mary Pickford, The*, 172

*Klim Sangin* (Gorky), 163

Knopf, Alfred A., Inc., 161

*Kolokol (The Bell)*, 158

Kolomenskoe, 31–32

Kondrashev, Boris, 132

Korolenko, Vladimir, 132

Kramer, Stanley, 166

*Krokodil*, 44, 77, 103–4

Kropotkin, Peter, 24

Ku Klux Klan, 42, 44

Kuleshov, Lev, 100

Lakier, Alexander, 52, 94, 193

*Last of the Mohicans, The* (Cooper), 11

Las Vegas Symphony Orchestra, 165
La Vieille Russie, 146–47
Law of Surplus Value, 73
Ledyard, John, 88–89
Leigh, Janet, 82
Lend-Lease program, 29, 32, 37
Lenin, V. I., 43, 63, 64, 66, 195
Leningrad, 137, 203–4
Leningrad-Helsinki train, 85–86
*Leningrad Postman, The* (Marshak), 174, 176
*Leningrad Symphony,* 29
Leo Tolstoy Museum, 57
Lermontov, M. Y., 142
Lesovsky, Admiral, 29
Lewis, Sinclair, 168
Library of Congress, U.S., 146
Lincoln, Abraham, 98
Lissitzky, El, 135
literature, 154–60
    banned, 155–57
    pulp fiction and, 162, 167
    Soviet view of, 162–64
    *see also* writers
Litvinov, Maksim, 23, 26
Lomonosov, Mikhail, 27
London, Jack, 97
Louis, Joe, 97
Lunacharsky, Anatoly, 98
Lyalichi Palace, 201

McCarthy, Mary, 155
McDonald's, 14, 55
Mailer, Norman, 155
Malevich, Kazimir, 135
Maltz, Albert, 26
*Man from Fifth Avenue, The,* 125
Marshak, Samuel, 174, 176
Marx, Karl, 73
mass culture, American, 166–67, 168–70, 172–76
Mayakovsky, Vladimir, 18, 25,

63, 93, 98, 119, 131, 134, 135, 195
*Meeting at a Far Meridian* (Wilson), 26
Mellon, Andrew, 146
Melville, Herman, 158
*Members of the City Troop and other Philadelphia Soldiery,* 192–93
Mendeleev, Dmitri, 192
*Merry-making at a Wayside Inn,* 193
Mickey Mouse festival, 173–75
Mikoyan, Anastas, 53–54, 146
Milestone, Lewis, 102
Miller, Arthur, 26, 153
Miller, Henry, 155
Minersville, Mo., 38–39
Ministry of Physical Culture, 16
model, America as, 13, 18
    abandonment of, 17, 18, 19
    ambivalence toward, 92–93
    for architecture, 135–37
    for consumer goods, 74–76
    distortions and subversions of, 53–54, 65–66
    for economy, 50, 54, 60
    for efficiency, 52, 92
    law of unequal development and, 72
    for management techniques, 63–64, 67, 68
modernity, 72, 134
Molotov, Vyacheslav, 158–59
Moscow, 13, 129–30, 136–37
Moscow Art Theater, 76, 119
*Moscow News,* 185–86
Moscow-St. Petersburg railway, 90
*Moskovskie novosti,* 76–77
Museum of Contemporary Art, 170–71

# Index

music, musicians, 13, 26, 139, 140, 141, 153, 165, 166, 167, 171
American popular, 168–70
*see also* jazz
"Music USA" (Voice of America), 141
myths, 12, 16
origins of, 51–52, 179–80
*see also* images of America

Nabokov, Vladimir, 90, 147, 148–52
Nader, Ralph, 117
Nearing, Scott, 26
*Nedelya*, 87, 133, 136, 195
Neiman Marcus, 79, 80
Nekrasov, Victor, 24–25
Nevsky Prospect, Leningrad, 130, 137
"New America" (Blok), 134
newspapers, 108
*Newsweek*, 22
New York, N.Y., 132–33, 135–137
*New York Times*, 73, 166
Niagara Falls, 122–23, 125
Nicholas I, 55, 90
Nicholas II, 146
*Night Life in Philadelphia*, 191, 192, 194
Nizhny Novgorod automobile plant, 61
Nixon, Richard M., 26
Nobel oil company, 201
*normalno*, 41–42, 43, 45

*Old Man and the Sea, The* (Hemingway), 158–59
Oltarzhevsky, Vyacheslav, 137
Olympics (1972), 198
"150,000" (Mayakovsky), 98

"100%" (Mayakovsky), 93
*One-Story America* (Ilf and Petrov), 120–24, 125
openness to life, as American virtue, 97
organizational skills, 68–72, 93
Osage Trust Lands, Kans., 39
*Our Hospitality*, 172
Overeaters Anonymous, 110

painters, 139, 144, 145, 146, 154
America as viewed by, 191–95
innovative, 170, 171
Palace of Soviets, 135
Pamyat Movement, 183
*Paragon*, 51
Paramount, 196
parochialism, 24–25
Pasternak, Alexander, 134–35
*Peace to the Newborn*, 101
Pedagogical Institute, 9
*Pennsylvania Gazette*, 27
people-to-people diplomacy:
etiquette in, 181–82, 192–99
model for, 199
national characteristics and, 181–92
permissiveness, as American quality, 72
personal guilt vs. social shame, 115
Peter the Great, 72, 182
Petrov, Evgeny, 19, 52, 120–24, 125, 126, 132, 195
photographs, 124, 126–27
Pickford, Mary, 172
*Pikant-shou*, 74
Pilnyak, Boris, 18, 108, 119, 195
*pinkertonovshchina*, 167
Pioneer youth groups, 15–16
places, physical and symbolic nature of, 128–33

# Index

Plato, 127
Poe, Edgar Allan, 97
political institutions, American:
    disparagement of, 40–43
    respect for, 38–40
*Poor Richard's Almanac* (Franklin),
    27, 96
pop psychology, 71
*Possessed, The* (Dostoevsky),
    193–94
Post, Marjorie Merriweather,
    146
Potemkin, Georgi, 105–6
Potemkin Villages, 80
pragmatism, 90–95
*Pravda*, 11, 30, 61, 62, 76, 97,
    120, 172
Presley, Elvis, 13
pretentiousness, as American
    fault, 194, 195
pride, 24, 25–26
privileges, to American visitors,
    185, 187
Progressive Commune, Cedar-
    vale, Kans., 38, 39
Project Kuzbas, 65–66, 186
propaganda, Soviet:
    in Cold War era, 13, 36, 40,
    62, 155
    on consumerism, 75–76, 77
    racism and, 43–47
    *see also* ideology
proper behavior, *see* behavior,
    proper
publishers, 158, 161–64
Pushkin, Alexander, 40, 94, 164
Pushkin Museum, 100
Pushkin Square, McDonald's on,
    55
Pushkin Theater, 174
Pyanov, Boris, 103–5
Pyatigorsk, 141–42

quality, 74, 77

racism, 40–47
Randolph, John, 92
Raphael, 146
reciprocity, 22–32
    American obtuseness and, 24,
    25, 30
    diplomatic relations and, 23–
    24, 25–26
    insensitivity and, 24, 30–31
    in Tsarist regimes, 28–29
    World War II, 29, 32–33
recruitment, worker, 64–66
*Red Sport*, 97
*Red Square in Summer*, 170
*Red Star, The*, 30
Reed, John, 26
Reid, Thomas Mayne, 90
Rembrandt, van Rijn, Paul, 146
Repin, Ilya, 144
restaurants, *see* food services;
    *specific restaurants*
Reunion Community, Miners-
    ville, Mo., 38–39
*Riders of the Purple Sage* (Grey),
    90
Riga Market, 82–83
Rimsky-Korsakov, N. A., 28
Ritchie, Joe, 68, 70
Robbins, Harold, 167
Robeson, Paul, 153
*Robin Hood*, 172
rock concerts, 168–71
Roerich, Nicholas, 144
Roosevelt, Franklin D., 32, 98
Roosevelt administration, 23–
    24
Rothschild oil company, 201
Russian national character, 57–
    58, 107–16, 181
    *sobornost* in, 114–16

Russian national character
(*cont.*)
social decorum and, 191–98
social structure and, 49–50

St. Louis World's Fair (1904),
144
St. Petersburg, 130, 182–83
St. Petersburg Academy of Sciences, 27, 28
Salinger, J. D., 158, 159
*samizdat* translations, 149,
155
Schwarzenegger, Arnold, 82
Scott, John, 185
self-assurance, as American virtue, 97
Sequoia National Park, 123
shared destiny concept, 16–20,
31
Sheremetyovo Airport, 67, 85
Shostakovich, Dmitri, 29
similarities between America and
Russia, 16–19, 91, 100, 103,
181
Simmons, Richard, 15, 16
Simonov, Konstantin, 102
simplicity, 96, 98, 100, 101, 102–
103, 104–5
sincerity, 32–33, 100
Singer, Paris, 137
Singer Sewing Machine Company, 137, 138
"sister cities," 180
skyscrapers, 133–37
slackers, 49–50, 57
Slavophilism, 183
Smelyakov, Nikolai, 120
smiling, 87–88
*sobornost*, 114–16
sociability, as American virtue,
191

social decorum:
gaffes in, 196
historical evolution and, 192
ideology and, 195, 198
model for, 199
*see also* behavior, proper
Socialist Realism, 137, 170, 171
Society for Technological Aid to
Soviet Russia, 64
*Sodom and Gomorrah*, 172
Solzhenitsyn, Aleksandr, 149,
156, 158, 183
*Something Happened* (Heller), 163
*Sophisticated Ladies*, 13, 139–41,
144
Sorokin, Pitirim, 93
soul, Russian, 90, 95, 116, 154,
183
Soviet Society of Designers, 77–
81
Soviet Union, *see specific topics*
Soviet Writers Union, 75
sports, 97
good manners in, 197–99
morality and, 198
"socialist," 198
*SShA (USA)*, 95
*Stagecoach*, 173
Stakhanov, Alexey, 66
Stalin, Joseph, 54, 92, 136, 157
Stallone, Sylvester, 82
Stanislavsky, Konstantin, 119
*Stars and Death*, 40, 41
Statue of Liberty, 119
Steffens, Lincoln, 26, 139, 153
*Stenka Razin, an Ataman of the
Bandits in the Reign of Aleksei
Mikhailovich*, 93
stereotypes of America, 12, 13,
35, 130–33, 200
*see also* American national
character; images of America

Stewart, James, 172
*stimbot*, 51–52
Stokowski, Leopold, 139
straight-talking, as American
    trait, 97, 98
students, 32–37
"Suprematist Building Among
    American Skyscrapers"
    (Malevich), 135
Svinin, Pavel, 16, 51, 191, 192–93

Taganka Theater, 40
Tchaikovsky, Peter, 108–9, 194
Tchaikovsky Competition, 26
"telebridges," 180
television, 72
    Americans as viewed in, 124–
    125, 127
tennis, 198
Texas, 132
    theater productions in, 13,
    139–43, 148–52
Thompson, William Boyce, 145
*Thousand Miles in Search of a
    Soul, A*, 12
*Time Forward* (Kataev), 186
Titian, 146
tobacco, 72
Tolstoy, Leo, 98, 108
topography, American, 133–37
tourist watchers, 72–73
Tracy, Spencer, 172
tradition, Russian, 53–54, 70
    of artistic categories, 167
    economic change and, 57–58
    family's role in, 112
    shame vs. guilt in, 115
    soul vs. detail in, 90
    tenacity of, 53–54, 57–58, 71
"transatlantic republic," 15
*Travel by Stage Coach near Tren-
    ton*, 193

travel restrictions, 117, 126–27
travel writers, 118–24
"Trenton, The," 56, 57
Trotsky, Leon, 158, 202
Truman, Harry S, 33
Turgenev, Ivan, 87
Twain, Mark, 17, 26, 87, 98–
    99

union, filmmakers, 58
United States, *see specific topics*
Updike, John, 153, 159

Van Doren, Mark, 139
*Vaudeville Dance*, 195
*Venus with Mirror* (Titian), 146
Vereshchagin, V. V., 144
visitors, American, 72–73, 88–
    89, 181–82
    blacks as, 43
    on business, 14
    celebrity, 15, 184
    in cultural exchange, 139, 153
    factory workers and techni-
    cians as, 64–66, 182–87
    as "presence," 13–14, 60
    privileges afforded to, 185–87
    as Soviet residents, 188–91
    tourist mentality of, 184
    treatment of, 183–91
Voice of America, 11, 141, 142
Vonnegut, Kurt, 168
Vyazemsky, P. A., 55, 56

Warhol, Andy, 168
Washington, D.C., 130, 132
Wayne, John, 173
Westinghouse, 62
Whistler, James, 154
Whistler, Robert, 90
*White Chief, The*, 90
Whitman, Walt, 98

Wilson, Edmund, 181–82
Wilson, Meredith, 26, 158
Wilson, Woodrow, 97–98
*Women's Wear Daily*, 73
worker psychology, 63–64, 66–
    67
workplaces, 63, 66–67, 68–72
World War II, 29–31, 32–33, 36,
    37
writers:
    American, 17, 26, 87, 97–99,
        139, 148–52, 154–60, 162,
        163, 167, 181
    Russian, 40, 87, 94, 98, 108,
        118–24, 125, 142, 174, 193–
        194
Wyeth, Andrew, 99–100

xenophobia, 183, 185–86

Zaitsev, Serge, 73
*Za rulyom (Behind the Wheel)*, 62
Zelyony Teatr (The Green Thea-
    ter), 168–69
Zhvanetsky, Mikhail, 133
ZIL car, 61
*Znamya*, 120
Zverlov, Peter, 69–71, 93